D1304628

Guide to the Best
in
Contemporary Piano Music

*An Annotated List of Graded Solo Piano Music
Published Since 1950*

Volume II: Levels 6 through 8

by
STANLEY BUTLER

The Scarecrow Press, Inc.
Metuchen, N. J.   1973

Library of Congress Cataloging in Publication Data

Butler, Stanley, 1914-
  Guide to the best in contemporary piano music.

    CONTENTS: v. 1. Levels 1 through 5.--v. 2. Levels
  6 through 8.
    1. Piano music--Bibliography--Graded lists.
  I. Title.
  ML132.P3BS8   016.7864'05'2   73-5693
  ISBN 0-8108-0628-2 (v. 1)
  ISBN 0-8108-0669-X (v. 2)

FOR CELIA

who first had the idea

TABLE OF CONTENTS

PREFACE

Most of the piano students whom I first hear as entering college freshmen have little experience with contemporary music. Yet when I have carefully chosen such a work for a student, the response invariably has been enthusiastic. I am convinced that students may be more ready for contemporary music than their teachers. Many of us certainly need suggestions as to what available literature will suit our particular needs.

To further test my assumption, I conducted a day's workshop at my own university with music from American publishers. I was amazed at the number who came. Later I led sessions at two music teachers' conventions on the same subject. The response, including a number of requests for additional lists of contemporary piano music which I had distributed at the conventions, convinced me that teachers and performers were ready and eager for a selection of the better works from the mass of music published.

Fortunately I had a sabbatical leave the next year from Willamette University. I headed for Europe with letters to European publishers. The response to requests for complimentary music made mail deliveries very exciting. The response also, unfortunately, kept my wife busy wrapping and returning music of little value. Little by little I culled music from the mail deliveries and from visits to dealers, publishers, and libraries. After two months in Paris and three months in London the accumulation of music partially examined made 20 bulky packages to mail home. And to that was added more music, obtained through personal contact with publishers in New York. Obviously I had my work cut out for me for the next several years, examining and analyzing the music at my piano. How joyous have been the discoveries of fine new music!

I hope that GUIDE TO THE BEST IN CONTEMPORARY PIANO MUSIC (Volume II as well as Volume I) will suggest music which will be considered, loved, and finally assimilated naturally into piano teaching and performance. Easy access to music of approximately 125 publishers from 22 countries may present challenges to your music stores. If your store can't supply you, Joseph Boonin, Inc. and de Keyser Music will keep the music in stock. (See page 167 for ordering instructions.)

There are several bases upon which the music has been selected. Foremost, it must have revealed its expressiveness to me; it must be music which I myself would be glad to perform or give a student. It must be in the main stream of the diversely contemporary. Some of the works described are conservatively contemporary, and so labelled. I want to lure the unitiated performer into an acquaintance with contemporary music. I have considered works for prepared piano outside the spectrum. There are a few pieces with elements of improvisation or indeterminancy and a few with a method of performance or notation different from the traditional.

The works chosen for this Volume II range in difficulty from those for advanced intermediates in level (or grade) 6 through the advanced level. Grading is indeed hazardous. I have tried to be consistent. Some idea of the difficulty of each level is suggested by comparison with the following well-known titles:

(Level 1: Kabalevsky SONG, from TWENTY-FOUR LITTLE PIECES, Op. 39)
(Level 3: Bartók TEASING SONG, from FOR CHILDREN, vol. 2)
(Level 5: Satie GYMNOPEDIE IN C)
Level 6: Shostakovich FANTASTIC DANCE, Op. 1, No. 1
Level 7: Ravel PAVANNE POUR UNE INFANTE DEFUNTE
Level 8: Griffes THE WHITE PEACOCK, from FOUR ROMAN SKETCHES, Op. 7.

I am most grateful to the publishers who have given me complimentary music. Without their cooperation the two volumes of this GUIDE would have been impossible. While I hoped to review all works published from 1950 through 1968 which suit my bases, this has obviously been impossible. There must be omissions in my own research or incomplete exposure of publications by some publishers. I apologize to

those composers whose published works I didn't see. However, I have been astonished to discover approximately 825
titles (357 in levels 6 through 8), among about 3000 examined,
worthy of performance. How heartening that composers will
work for love, knowing there will be sketchy monetary return! And it is encouraging, indeed, that the gambling
spirit is still alive in publishers.

Regrettably, users of this GUIDE may be thwarted
occasionally from purchasing a title because it is out of
print temporarily or permanently. Every effort has been
made to insure each work's availability up to June, 1972.
Since prices vary, none have been included.

In addition to publishers' personnel, help has come
from many sources. Election as an Atkinson Fellow at
Willamette University gave me the opportunity to pursue
problems in analysis. A grant from the Shell Oil Assists
Fund, administered by Willamette University's Dr. Harry
Manley, helped defray expenses. Practical assistance
came from Wills Music Store, Wiltsey-Weathers Music and
Berkeley Music House.

My friend Dorothy Butler edited the entire manuscript. Charles Bestor, former dean of the College of
Music at Willamette University, not only assisted with
some analyses but also gave generous counsel in practical
matters, as did Mr. Ralph Wright, assistant to the presi-
dent for university relations. Professors Gerald Kechley
and Ellis Kohs helped me clarify many a problem. John
Wiser at Joseph Boonin's gave experienced advice. Help
also came from Acting Dean Richard Stewart and Professors Raul Casillas, Paula Drayton, Clarence Kraft, Otto
Mandl, Bruce McIntosh, Marion Morange, William New-
man, Joseph Schnelker, Robert Stoltze, Monte Tubbs,
Marija Udris, Julio Viamonte, and Mr. Ladislav Bazdek,
and Mr. Bennet Ludden.

It is a mystery to me how typist, teacher, and
student Audrey Hultgren was able to decipher my manuscript.

Finally, my wife Celia not only endured my preoccu-
pation but actively participated in many ways.

Stanley Butler
Willamette University
February, 1973

HOW TO USE THIS GUIDE

This GUIDE begins with Level 6 and continues through Level 8 (Volume I contains Levels 1 through 5). For easy reference, the entry number for each listing is the grade level of the piece followed by a number representing the order within that level. Thus, the first piece in Level 6 is 6.1. Compositions are generally listed alphabetically by composers in each level. Main entry titles are given in the original language when the editor provides no English title.

Collections of works by different composers are listed at the beginning of their prevailing level. Each accepted work in such collections is reviewed under the composer's name, indicated by a direction such as "see 6.44." When the entry is a collection by a single composer, the general tenor of the collection is appraised, but to save space, only about half the works are specifically described.

Other information included:

Year composition was written, if known.
Translation of titles from the original language to English; usually also translation of performance directions.
Abbreviation for specific publisher and the number for the work in the publisher's listing, if available, is placed in parentheses immediately following review of the work. (Full names of publishers and United States agent, when appropriate, are found in the publisher information section, page 168.) Date of publication and number of music pages follow publisher's name.
Number of pieces in collections.
Performance time, if indicated.
Fngr (fingering included).
MM (metronome marks included).

Ped (pedal directions included).

*Anal (analysis printed with music, asterisk denotes a particularly helpful one).

Biog (biography included).

Ch (music suitable only for children).

Numbers in parentheses preceding publisher information indicate the piece on that page is not recommended. See, for example the "(29.)" in entry 6. 56.

Final numbers at end of description of a collection signify the difficulty levels of entire collection when more than one level is included.

A title-plus-composer and composer-plus-title index is found on page 150. The index to musical and pianistic features on page 141 should be useful.

Technical words (such as "coupled writing") are explained in the glossary (page 138), unless they are defined in The Harvard Brief Dictionary of Music by Willi Apel and Ralph P. Daniel, published by Harvard University Press in hard cover and Amsco Music Company and Washington Square Press in soft cover. When foreign terms are not translated, Musician's Handbook of Foreign Terms, by Christine Ammer, published in soft cover by G. Schirmer (1971), will be helpful.

Note: citations are occasionally made to works that are included in Volume I of this work (e.g., "3.23" or "5.15"): full data for these works are given beginning on page 133.

ABBREVIATIONS

acc	accompaniment
Anal	analysis
Biog	biography
Ch	for children
E	E major
e	e minor
ed	editor, edited by
Fngr	fingering
LH	left hand
MM	metronome
Ped	pedal
p	page
pp	pages
RH	right hand

OUT-OF-PRINT SELECTIONS (I and II)

The following titles would have been included in volumes I or II had they not gone out-of-print.

Baird, Tadeusz. Sonatina nr 2 (PWM, 1953, 14 pp.)
Berlinski, Herman. Very Talkative (AMP, 1957, 2 pp.)
Berlinski, Herman. With Grace (AMP, 1957, 2 pp.)
Chanler, Theodore. A Child in the House (Merc, 1956, 21 pp.)
Diamond, David. The Tomb of Melville (Leeds, 1950, 5 pp.)
Distler, Hugo. Elf kleine Klavierstücke (Bär 1803, 1956, 15 pp.)
Duck, Leonard. Frescoes (Chap-L 1965, 18 pp.)
Fuller, Jeanne Weaver. Dorian Rondo (SB, 1964, 2 pp.)
George, Earl. Kangaroos! (Oxf, 1960, 2 pp.)
Geszler, György. Viz Hajtya a Malmot (EMB, 1958, 10 pp.)
Haufrecht, Herbert. Quasi Ostinato (AMP, 1956, 4 pp.)
Holoubek, Ladislav. Detské Hry a Radosti (Shv, 1964, 13 pp.)
Járdányi, Pal. Rondo (EMB, 1958, 4 pp.)
Jirák, K. B. 12 Piano Pieces for Children, Op. 62, Book 1 (AMP, 1953, 12 pp.)
Kardos, Dezider. Bagately, Op. 18 (Shv, 1966, 24 pp.)
Lees, Benjamin. Kaleidoscopes (B&H, 1959, 13 pp.)
Le Fleming, Christopher. Sunday Morning and Whistling Tune (Oxf, 1963, 4 pp.)
Lloyd, Norman. Three Scenes from Memory (EV, 1963, 6 pp.)
McKay, George Frederick. Explorations, Volume 2 (JF, 1965, 18 pp.)
Mailman Martin. Petite Partita (Mil-NY, 1961, 5 pp.)
Murrill, Herbert. Sonatina (Oxf, 1953, 12 pp.)
Novák, Milan. 1. Klavírna Suita (Shv, 1964, 26 pp.)
Parík, Ivan. Tri Klavírne Skladby (Shv, 1963, 11 p.)
Pitfield, Thomas B. Toccatina (Oxf, 1960, 4 pp.)

Sacco, P. Peter. <u>Procession</u> (SB, 1964, 3 pp.)

<u>Slovenská Klavírna Tvorba</u>, 1962 (Shv, 1962, 33 pp.)

<u>Slovenská Klavírna Tvorba</u>, 1966 (Shv, 1966, 46 pp.)

Szabó, Ferenc. <u>Toccata</u> (EMB, 1964, 7 pp.)

Tardos, Béla. <u>Miniatures</u> (EMB, 1962, 8 pp.)

Toch, Ernst. <u>Three Little Dances</u>, Op. 85 (Mil-NY, 1962, 6 pp.)

Wigham, Margaret. <u>Festivals</u> (SB, 1955, 3 pp.)

LEVEL 6

6.1 British Piano Music, Contemporary.
Collection of fine twelve-tone works. (See 6.44, 6.61 and 8.80.) Contains music by Banks, Fricker, Hamilton, and Searle. (Scho 10547, 1956, 27 pp.) 8 pieces, 4 composers. Some MM & Ped. 6, some 7 & 8.

6.2 Bulgarian Piano Music, Contemporary, Book 2, ed by Otto Daube.
Four pieces reviewed (see 6.81, 6.91 and 7.36), three are easily accessible. Contains music by Goleminov, Kasandjiev, Kürktschijski, Ikonomov, and Wladigerov. Introduction and biographies in English and German, titles also in Bulgarian. (HG, 1965, 13 pp.) 6 pieces. Some Fngr, MM, Ped. *Biog. 6, some 7.

6.3 Japanese Folk Air(s) on the Piano.
Sympathetic arrangements of melodies by Itō, Koyama, Makino, and Tsukatani. All pieces reviewed. (See 5.151, 6.76, 6.89 and 6.101.) Fine balance between literal statements of melody and pianistic additions in spirit of melody. Melodies, in a pentatonic scale with usually two half steps, are almost always in treble. Cluster elements in accs, with substitutions for third of chord. Commentaries by composers in Japanese offer sociological background and analysis. (Zen, 1960, 47 pp.) 13 pieces. Some MM. *Anal. 6, some 4, 5, 7 & 8.

6.4 New Music for the Piano, ed by Joseph Prostakoff.
Remarkable collection of works by thoroughly contemporary American composers, majority born since 1910. Value of collection enhanced by a skillful recording by Robert Helps on 2-album LSC--7042 (stereo) and RCA Victor Red Seal. Booklet of biographies included with recordings. Works by seventeen of the twenty-four

15

composers are reviewed. (See 6.15, 6.52, 6.67, 6.83,
6.86, 6.122, 7.4, 7.8, 7.74, 7.77, 7.93, 8.13, 8.16,
8.40, 8.45, 8.63 and 8.71.) Music by five of the re-
maining six composers are too difficult for this GUIDE.
Contains music by Adler, Alexander, Babbitt, Bacon,
Berger, Berkowitz, Brunswick, Cazden, Dahl, V. Fine,
Gideon, Glanville-Hicks, Gould, Helps, Hovhaness,
Kennan, Kim, Kraft, Overton, Perle, Pisk, Powell,
Prostakoff, and Weber. (LG, 1963, 105 pp.) 35
pieces, 24 composers. Some MM, Ped. 6, 7 & 8.

6.5   Nordisk Klavermusik, Ny.
New Northern Piano Music contains sonatinas by three
Danish, two Finnish, one Norwegian, and six Swedish
composers. Eight works reviewed. (See 4.127, 5.119,
6.14, 6.94, 6.97, 7.96, 8.12 and 8.43.) Contains
music by Bentzon, Bergman, de Frumerie, Høffding,
von Koch, Larsson, Lidholm, Palmgren, Riisager,
Rosenberg, Saeverud and Wirén. Included are pictures of composers, biography in composer's native
language, and comments by composer on the music.
(Geh, 1951, 133 pp.) 13 sonatinas, 12 composers.
Some MM & Ped. Biog. 6 & 8, some 4, 5 & 7.

6.6   Pepparrot, ed by Birgitta Nordenfelt.
Fine variety in Horseradish (title has only personal
significance), subtitled New Scandinavian Piano Music.
Eight works reviewed. (See 4.122, 5.82, 6.17,
6.63, 6.65, 6.96, 6.130 and 6.131.) Most works are
tonal and fairly conservative. Contains music by
Blomdahl, Bäck, Holmboe, Høffding, Lidholm, Riisager,
and Saeverud. Foreword, biographies and titles in
Swedish, English, and German. (Nord, 1951, 37 pp.)
16 pieces, 7 composers. Usually Fngr & MM, some
Ped. Biog. 6, some 4 & 5.

6.7   Soviet Piano Music, Contemporary, Book 1, ed by
      Rudolf Lück.
Quite accessible. Six of seven works published after
1950 reviewed. (See 6.103, 6.104, 6.151, 6.170,
7.7 and 8.81.) Curiously varied volume includes
romantic works, extrovert music for children, and
Schoenbergian works. Contains music by Babadshanjan,
Glière, Kabalevski, Khachaturian, Mamissaschwili,
Marguste, Pärt, Silwestrow, Swiridow, and Zytowitsch.
Discerning foreword and biographies in English and

Level 6.8

German; titles also in Russian. (HG, 1968, 23 pp.)
10 pieces. Some Fngr, MM & Ped. *Biog. 6,
some 7 & 8.

6.8 ADAMIS, MICHAEL. Epitymbio (1965).
On a Tomb is a solemn study in sonority with economical means. Mildly clashing seconds and other
near-cluster combinations. Wide range. No melody.
Twelve-tone set gradually completed three times. (In
7.1, 2 pp.) MM, Ped.

6.9 APOSTEL, H. E. Suite "Concise," Op. 24.
Programmatic pieces give composer's charming and
witty musical impressions of visit to Swiss village of
Concise. Varied articulation. Both polyphonic and
homophonic texture, latter predominating. Forms clear.
Twelve-tone influence. The Promenade (II) has frisky
short slurs and small leaps. Motives recur. Often
in two voices. Invertible counterpoint present. Harmonically interesting Greetings (IV) is theme with six
short variations and coda. In theme, four motives,
each associated with main characters involved in visit,
are presented. Composer's motive has tones from his
initials (b natural standing for German H). Variations
are free. Third has declamatory octaves, fourth has
light fleeting scales, often of whole tones. Coda begins like the theme. In Dodecaphonic Problem (V) the
same tone set is stated once in each of its transformations, melody alone; first the original order is heard,
then its inversion, retrograde, and inversion of the
retrograde. Between each statement of very different
contours is similar material of irregular twelve-tone
writing. Departure (VII) is Arrival (I) virtually back-
wards. Translations are The House (III) and The Wine
and the Fish (VI). (UE 12512, 1956, 13 pp.) 7 pieces,
11 min. 6 & 7.

6.10 AUBIN, TONY. Caprice Pastoral.
Charming Allegretto, appealing to the performer sensitive to "quiet statement [and] able to distinguish calm-
ness from dulness...." Pastel harmonic explorations,
particularly in treble register. Equal hand emphasis.
Splendid acc variety, such as scale figurations, LH
varied arpeggios, and RH broken sixths. Fine study
for melody and acc in same hand. Moderate number
of ornaments, with directions to begin "on the beat."
(In 5.1, 4 pp.) MM, Ped.

6.11 BABBITT, MILTON. Semi-Simple Variations.
Title seems sly acknowledgment of music's complexity.
Detailed dynamic directions for expressionistic twelve-
tone music.   At least half beats will need to be
counted; "rhythmically, the sixteenth notes in the first
six measures represent all 16 possible partitions of
the quarter note in terms of the 16th note unit." Concentrated measures contain much of the contemporary.
(Pr, 1957, 2 pp.) Fngr, MM, Ped. *Anal.

6.12 BACEWICZ, GRAŻYNA. Maly Tryptyk na Fortepian.
Pieces of Little Triptych for Piano are studies in sonority.   Texture often thick with long damper pedal.
I and III are organized similarly--each begins and ends
with wide ranging stabs in which trills or cluster ac-
cumulations are prevalent; rapid polyharmonic passage
work in each middle section.   II has vivid dynamics.
Uses three tone sets consecutively; each first emphasizes one interval and ends with cluster or pedal-tone
element.   Usually one-line music.   (PWM, 1966, 5
pp.) 3 pieces. 2 min, 6 sec. MM, Ped. 6 & 7.

6.13 BADINGS, HENK. Sonate No. 3 (1944).
Beautifully balanced neo-classic work, modest in its
successfully fulfilled aspiration.   Usually in treble
range.   First and last movements are in overtone
mode on C with few deviations.   Each hand often has
double notes, particularly thirds.   Rhythm and texture
conservative.   First Allegro in closely knit sonata
form with compact motive development.   Many two-
note slurs.   Each hand has rapid passage work, including some extensions.   Lento is deeply morose.   In
G, with chromaticism.   Repeat of melody ornate.
Closing Allegretto, resembling first movement, has
much simple variation of material.   (Don, 1961, 13
pp.) 3 movements. MM, some Ped.

6.14 BENTZON, NIELS VIGGO. Sonatine, Op. 62 (1950).
Music at first seems full of surprises, yet unity reveals itself.   Ideas follow each other fluently.   Real
dash is present even though the work is not profound.
Allegro has an ear-teasing ease of harmonic change in
a tonal framework.   Fluent passage work for each
hand bears some relationship to traditional writing.
Varied repetition of material.   Interval of fourth prominent.   In the solemn Andante tranquillo, dense added-
note chords alternate with single notes which are pre-

ceded by short quick flurries "played before the beat."
Extrovert Rondo shows Hindemith influences; material
alternates with lighter, effective figures divided between hands. (In 6.5, 10 pp.) 3 movements. MM.
Biog.

6.15 BERGER, ARTHUR. Two Episodes: 1933.
Sensitive and discreet twelve-tone works. Articulation
greatly varied. Many different performance directions.
Shorter and simpler I moderately fragmented. Has directions like "sonoro rubato e teneramente," "tempo
guisto," "sub. secco," and "sub. misterioso." Allegro
molto moderato II is in ABA form, with second A
changed some. Opening twelve-tone set acts as motto.
Primarily in two voices, thinning to coupled writing,
or thickening to double notes. Mostly dolce. (In 6.4,
4 pp.) MM, Ped. 6 & 8.

6.16 BERGMAN, ERIK. Intervalles, Op. 34 (1949).
Wit and intelligence in primarily scherzando, energetic
moods. Using both melodic and harmonic seconds
through octaves, each Interval ingeniously exploits one
interval. Much motive manipulation. Collection includes studies for hand and forearm staccato, trills and
meter changes. Vivace I, with seconds or inversions
(sevenths), has deftly placed slurs and accents used
over wide range. Usually soft. Neo-classic. IV is
a fascinating "sotto voce fantastico" with perfect fifths.
Often coupled writing and all-treble or bass range.
VII is an Allegro energico with rapid hand alternation.
Octaves or unisons, sometimes repeated, exploited.
Irregular accents and effective forward motion devices
give drama to the perpetual motion. (Faz, 1964, 24
pp.) 7 pieces. 6 & 7.

6.17 BLOMDAHL, KARL-BIRGER. Litet Tema med Variationer.
Simple Theme with Variations is splendidly conceived.
Sturdy theme progresses through six variations with effective variety. In d, but first ten tones of theme are
always different. Theme is in bass, doubled by fourths
or octaves, inverted, rhythmically changed, etc.
Many double notes. (In 6.6, 2 pp.) Fngr, MM. Biog.

6.18 BRADSHAW, SUSAN. Eight Hungarian Melodies (1953).
Attractive tunes in imaginative settings. Low bass
tones judiciously used to create fullness of sound.

Melody always in RH.   Often chromatic motion in acc.
Vivace staccato tune of III is in pure a aeolian.   LH
forearm staccato acc related to an Alberti bass.   For
second setting, tune's note lengths remain the same,
but with more exact rhythmic scanning, meters shifting between 3/4 and 2/4.   LH has low tones involving
quick shifts.   Appealing 5/8 melody of Allegretto IV
is set in two ways: first in two voices and then in
much fuller texture including octaves.   Harmony for
modal tune quite exploratory in second setting.   Melody for the mournful Lento V is in e-flat aeolian.   After chromatic acc line settles in E-flat, tune harmonized second time in B.   Then a low bass dirgelike
acc emphasizes major sevenths and minor seconds.
Lively intricate rhythm found in VI.   Tune has two
measures of 8/8 and two of 7/8.   Acc, adding one or
two voices, has ties through beginning of rhythmic
groupings and sprinkling of three equal tones spread
across two beats, or the opposite.   (Ches, 1961, 8
pp.)   8 min.   MM.   6, some 5 & 7.

6.19   BRESGEN, CESAR.   Balkan Impressions, Vol. 2.
Authenticity and fantasy heard in settings of folk songs
and dances from Rumania, Albania, and Hungary.   "In
many of these pieces these melodies appear in a
simple arrangement, but in others they are used purely as the foundation for a freer form of composition."
Accs often have drone elements.   Titles and foreword
in English and German.   Four-measure mixolydian
melody of Christmas Song, with haunting medieval fla-
vor, repeated in six settings.   Three settings have
more active RH counter melody, once in an inner
voice.   Dance (p. 26), with many very Allegro notes,
is spontaneous and splendidly crafted.   LH acc includes
sparse rhythmic chords (sometimes on off-beats) and
forearm staccato broken chords.   Allegro Albanian
Dance builds to treble screech and then subsides.
Many augmented seconds in melody of small intervals.
Has octaves and various ostinatos.   Virtuoso, fanciful
Hungarian Bagpipe (nearly four pages) has energetic
drive increasing toward the end with rhythms of two
against three.   Many drone bass patterns using rapid
hand and finger staccato.   (Lit/Pet 5967b, 1964, 16
pp.)   10 pieces.   Some Fngr, MM.   4, 5, 6 & 7.

6.20   BRUSCHETTINI, MARIO.   Sonatina.
Typically Italian in accessibility.   Uncomplicated neo-

classicism. Consistent, with no contemporary problems. Allegro con brio is fluent and natural. Excellent training for rapid legato passage work with both
hands. Traditional form. In C with almost no key
contrast. Calme e dolce movement is undemonstra-
tively lyrical. Usually three voices, treble leading.
Closing Moderato has irresistible rondo spirit. Constant dotted rhythms. F and p contrasts. (Ric,
1955, 8 pp.) 3 movements. Some Fngr & MM. Ch.
6, some 5.

6.21 BURKHARD, WILLY. Six Preludes, Op. 99.
Writing of decided character. Much variety: in addition to works described in detail, Adagio II has polyrhythms, III is a two-voice etudelike perpetual motion
with kaleidoscopic chromatic harmonies, and IV uses
all twelve tones for the subject of a four-voice ricer-
care-style work. Allegro agitato I is in virtuoso toccata style. Beginning with coupled writing, it pulls
away from such unity to dissonance and then to a fuller
texture. Broadly tonal. V is a whispering, impressionistic Moderato using rapid hand alternation in the
manner of a "harp-like soft tremolo." Amid constant
sounds washed together by pedal, a few tenuto treble
tones vaguely emerge as melody. VI is an incredibly
varied Andante based on twelve-tone set of fifths and
fourths. New texture at almost every beginning of the
set, from numerous one-line passages to an arpeggiated chord of all twelve tones. Set is often transposed, also used in retrograde. (Bär 3504, 1956, 11
pp.) MM. 6, 7 & 8.

6.22 CASTILLO, RICARDO. Eight Preludes.
Miniatures charmingly capture sensitive moods in a
few measures. Pastel colorings of impressionism.
Motto is "My soul has its secret, my life has its
mystery." Tonal. Brief biography in Spanish. III,
IV and V should be played as a unit. Conservative.
I, a delicate "merry" Presto reminiscent of Debussy,
glistens with slight dissonances. RH rapid ostinato
acc is practice for weaker fingers. II, a Lento
marked "with anguish," has much expression in few
tones. VI an inventively fluent Allegretto marked mf
and giocoso. Chromatic continuous sixteenth note motion; LH acc often a tremolo. VII is "decisive,"
"very rhythmic," and "guisto." LH acc in traditional
"back and forth" pattern covering a tenth. (HE, 1957,

11 pp.) 6 & 7, some 5.

6.23 CASTILLO, RICARDO. Suite in D.
Gentle and graceful with Frenchlike suavity. Simpler
than it sounds. Pianistic, with many broken intervals,
often fourths. Singing quality needed. Incidental polyharmonies. II is bewitching with polyrhythms--lyrical
treble melody in 3/4 and extended broken chord acc in
6/8. Slight encounters with dissonances like added-
note chords. Also fourth chords. III, marked Moderato, has expressive purity. In a aeolian or C with
only two accidentals. Opening melody appears in widely-spaced coupled writing; melodies often outline chords.
Faster middle section has rotary motion, Alberti sounding acc for both hands. IV is a lovely Cantabile andantino. Usually in two voices, LH accompanying.
Mildly tinted coloring from modulations. (PAU, 1957,
11 p.) 5 movements. MM. Biog. 6 & 7.

6.24 CASTRO, JOSÉ MARÍA. Diez Piezas Breves (1932).
Ten Short Pieces capture with splendid precision popular South American elements or abstract tone play.
Musically sophisticated. Tonal. Printed from reasonably legible manuscript. Study (1) is sparkling perpetual motion in treble register. Slurred recurring major
seventh adds gentle brightness. Each hand has rapid
tremolos. Allegretto Danza bewitches with its rhythmic mixture of two and three and its flirtation with
polyharmonies. Circus (6) captures with sure craft
spontaneous, raucous, and kaleidescopic moods. Moderate leaps. Mood of Funeral March of the Sad Creole (7) depicted by traditional dotted rhythms, a low
bell tolling, and expressive rests. In Bells (10) the
air is filled with clanging fourths and with two peals--
one of ascending dotted strokes and the other of four
descending tones. Melodies have varied and resourceful settings. Realistic dissonance. Translations are
The Fountain (2), Cradle Song (3), Sorrowful Song (4),
Street Waltz (8), and Perpetual Motion (9). (Barry,
1955, 13 pp.) MM. 6 & 7, some 4 & 5.

6.25 COLIN, GEORGES. Cinque Croquis d'Élèves.
Distinctive melody featured in Five Sketches of Students. Excellent for legato finger explorations with
varied extensions. Usually no meter signatures.
Texture is thin, often in two voices. Tonal, with all
twelve tones very freely used. Capricious gains its

character largely from rhythmic changes and frequent
stops. Most difficult rhythm is three sixteenths followed by a triplet against two eighths. Pitch shape also greatly varied. Coquette is a delightful waltz, with
two-beat measures, etc. Angular melody. Tempo
gradually increases to prestissimo. French directions
in beginning of collection indicate: (1) accidentals ap-
ply only to note immediately following; (2) large notes
indicate note to be emphasized; (3) measure signs are
only an aid to the eye; and (7) never accent the first
note of a rhythmic group. Translations are Dreamer
(4) and Chatterer (5). (SF, 1962, 12 pp.) Fngr, some
MM. 6 & 7, some 5.

6.26 CONSTANTINIDIS, YANNIS. Greek Miniatures, Vol.
      III (1948-51).
Beautiful melodies stressed in settings true to folk
spirit. Tunes ingeniously depend much on fingers and
held tones for fullness. Many ornaments used. Often
modal. Irregular meters like 5/8 and 7/8. Sometimes
two pieces grouped together. Meticulous editing; exact pedaling, for instance. Modernisms are conservative. In Andante serio XXXV serious character emphasized by melody doubled two octaves lower and by parallel fifths. RH has many grace notes. Melody in
XXXVIII includes notated turns. Acc has an ostinatolike figure to which is sometimes added a secondary
voice. Lighthearted Allegro XXXIX follows attacca
from the preceding; acc is harmonically piquant with
augmented and other triads, preceded by acciaccaturas.
Equal hand emphasis. Acc in the mournful XLIII, often centering around subdominant, has considerable free-
dom with fifth, sixth and seventh tones of f aeolian
mode. Treble melody is pure aeolian. Many tones
held in acc. Work moves attacca to Allegretto vivo
XLIV, which captures giocoso feeling of 7/8 melody by
free treatment and imaginative acc. Melody adds ornaments, develops motives, or trails off into pianistic
play. Acc repeats tonic pedal to represent folk instrument drone. Variety between pedaled and secco settings. (Ron, 1957, 18 pp.) 14 pieces, 12 min. Fngr,
MM, Ped. 6 & 7, some 5.

6.27 CORTÉS, RAMIRO. The Genie of the Waters (1956).
Hauntingly expressive with fluid motion. Uses full keyboard range. Search for evocative tone quality is in-
herent in music's mystical nature. Broadly tonal. RH

has passage of weak finger melody and measured trill
acc with first and second fingers. (Pr, 1958, 3 pp.)
Fngr, MM, some Ped. *Anal.

6.28 COULTHARD, JEAN. White Caps.
Fluent and pianistic Vigoroso. Sharply articulated RH
melody, with syncopations and rests against perpetual
motion acc usually in LH. A rondo (from Sonatina)
with many technical uses: hands equally emphasized,
RH weak fingers strengthened in double notes, quick
hand alternation, and rapid hand staccato. Final tonic
chord with added second and raised fourth suggests
free tonal treatment. (BMI, 1955, 4 pp.) MM.

6.29 DAMASE, JEAN-MICHEL. Féeries, Op. 38.
Fairy Tales are pleasant vignettes; not profound, but
often chic in the French manner. Tonal, with many
seventh, ninth, and added-note chords, as well as other more sophisticated harmonies. Useful for reading
purposes, often using no key signatures and wide ranging with varied keyboard patterns. Particular pianistic
traits often evident in pieces. Conservative. Full-
textured Sleeping Beauty (1) uses parallel seventh
chords in one hand and parallel fourth chords in the
other. In D-flat. Fine opportunity for LH practice
of four-note chords. Cinderella (4) has much flat and
sharp variety. After an introduction it moves in the
"tempo of a minuet." RH has three and four-note
chords. Green Streamer (5) includes cadenzalike opening and pp presto motion alternating between the hands
in a high register. The Blue Bird (7) is charming in
its tinselly high register staccatos. LH acc has rapid
four-note broken chords and double note displacements.
Tuneful Tom Thumb (9) has rapidly repeated staccato
tones with the same finger. Chordal passages require
rotary technique. In Little Red Riding Hood (11) both
the little girl and the wolf are aptly portrayed. LH
has staccato broken tenths. Many accidentals in first
inversion seventh chords in The Deer in the Woods
(12). The White Cat (13) is cleverly characterized by
pp staccatos and nasty, high-register dissonances preceded by rapid RH purring grace notes. The Fairies
(16) has lush seventh chords. Useful chord displace-
ment study for both hands. Title translations are
Donkey Skin (2), Puss in Boots (3), Girl with Golden
Hair (6), The Sheep (8), Beauty and the Beast (10),
Ricky with the Tassel (14), and Gracieuse and Per-

cinet [people's names] (15). (HL, 1957, 21 pp.) 16
pieces. MM. 6 & 7, some 5.

6.30 DAVIES, PETER MAXWELL. Five Little Pieces
(1960, 1962, 1964).
Sensitive row-related works, discreet and economical.
No dynamic level above mf--much pp. Each piece divided into several sections, clarified by light double
bars; each has a recapitulation, disguised by rhythm
and spacing changes. First three gain unity within
themselves from signs of repeated bass line; all have
some recapitulation. Meter changes, such as shift
from 2/4 to 7/16. Care needed to keep voices clear
when one crosses another. (B&H, 1968, 4 pp.) MM.

6.31 DEBUSMAN, EMIL. Sonata No. I, Op. 17.
Merry neo-classic work. Very conservative. As
suave as French music. Pianistically facile writing.
Useful for developing speed with traditional patterns,
including repeated tones. Much hand staccato. Molto
allegro I is usually one-line music with alternating
hands. Harmonies in the Andante change by chromatic
motion in one or more voices. In a, like the other
movements, but with pedal tones on d, b-flat and e-
flat. Harmonies become more dissonant at fff climax.
Usually each hand plays double notes; RH includes awkward stretch of octaves plus seconds added to lower
tone. Dashing Presto has more repeated tones and difficult brief octave passages. Frequent cross relations
cause piquant harmonies. (AME, 1958, 15 pp.) 3
movements. MM. 6, 7 & 8.

6.32 DE LEEUW, TON. Cinq Études (1951).
Each of the Five Etudes is pleasant and composed with
a specific purpose. Equal hand emphasis. Neo-classic. Tonal with free use of all twelve tones. Care-
free Poco allegro I is "for repeated notes," usually
RH single and LH double or triple notes. Polytonal
suggestions. Usually in 5/8. Harmonic charm in IV
"for hands crossed," particularly LH over RH. Attractive contrast between beats divided by four and
three. Happy V, "for agility," provides practice in
matching tones for dynamic and rhythmic evenness.
Ingenious use of trills followed by scale passages with
no thumb under, alternating hands and scales together
by fifths, sixths, etc. II is "for unison" (coupled
writing) and III is "for the left hand," with extensions,

contractions, and finger substitution. (Don, 1951, 9
pp.) MM. 6, some 5 & 7.

6.33 DE LEEUW, TON. Lydische Suite.
Lydian Suite is pleasant, optimistic music. Splendid
for developing single note fluency. Traditional rhythms,
ranges, and piano style. Raised fourth of lydian mode
is constant, but opening Allegro also has lowered seventh (overtone scale) and Andante tranquillo lowered
third (Hungarian minor scale). Much treble range.
Second movement has a sonorous texture, contrasting
with thinner outer movements; it leads directly to a
merry, leggiero Vivace in the manner of the first
movement. RH melody often has scale patterns, LH
acc rapid broken chords. (Don, 1954, 9 pp.) 3
movements.

6.34 DUBOIS, PIERRE MAX. Esquisses.
Sketches are salon-type pieces with proverbial French
charm. Graceful music, relaxed and facile. Seventh
and ninth chords, chords with added seconds and sixths,
chromaticisms, brief modulations, and other harmonic
colorings. Felicitous piano writing. Conservative.
Pastourelle is attractive with ear-catching momentary
harmonic displacements. Has LH medium extensions
and RH weak finger melodies. The Village Woman (5)
is more direct and folklike than other pieces in collection. LH percussive acc may be grouped by three,
three, and two, while RH is in the most regular 2/4.
Tango rhythms are found in Cuban Sketch (7); also LH
broken chords (using fifth over first finger), and fine
dynamic variety. Momentary chromatic coloring. In
Mandolines (9) LH finger staccato and hand staccato for
both hands on repeated tones. Rustic Sketch (10) uses
broken tenths and arpeggios in LH and parallel thumb
tones on inner voice as well as parallel sixth chords
in RH. 6 is translated Intermezzo. (Led, 1961, 22
pp.) 10 pieces, 16 min. 6 & 7, some 5.

6.35 DUTILLEUX, HENRI. Blackbird.
Delightful novelty. A few realistic roulades are combined with many light staccatos to portray bird. Excellent for hand staccato in both hands. Constant rapid
motion. Translation of next to last direction is "clear,
but with a little pedal. " (In 5.1, 3 pp.) Some Fngr,
MM, some Ped.

6.36 DUTILLEUX, HENRI. Résonances.
Light and fanciful. Title depicted by different kinds of
writing: soft all major or all minor chords (sometimes with added second) punctuated by same type
chords half step away played either sforzando or as
broken grace notes; rapid toccatalike coupled writing
two octaves apart; contrary motion minor chords; and
melody with staccato broken chord acc. Footnote on
last page indicates RH chord is not repeated. (In 8.2,
4 pp.) Fngr, MM.

6.37 EGGE, KLAUS. Gukkoslåtten (1944).
Goathorn-Dance has an interesting and appropriate setting for few-note melody like a Norwegian folktune.
Has accent vigor. ABA in form, the last A lengthened considerably. LH acc in A usually offbeat; B is
slower. LH ninth reach. (Ly 252, 1953, 2 pp.)
Some MM & Ped.

6.38 EL-DABH, HALIM. Mekta' in the Art of Kita', Book
III.
Discreet pianistic effects blend imaginatively with East-
ern character--composer is Egyptian. Title could be
translated as "The Microcosm in the Art of Macro-
cosm." Further, to quote analysis printed in Books I
and II "titles of each individual piece primarily indicate the Iqa [rhythm] of each piece. Other meanings
are also implied by each title...." Hypnotic repetition
of small fragments. Unusual key signatures, often different in each hand. Samai ("triple rhythm, floridity
of movement, reflective") has heterophony. As a result there are momentary minor sevenths, major seconds, etc. Meters vary between 3/4 and 6/8, latter
sometimes unannotated. In Sayera ("duple rhythm...
lyrical") short-range dolce melody of varied articulation alternates with reiterated ff percussive bass
chords. Treble signature is f-sharp and b-flat; bass
is e-flat. Collection contains also Basseet ("duple
rhythm, simplicity of character, lightness, gaiety"),
Nawakht ("quintuple rhythm, richness and anxiety of
sound"), and Soufiane ("complex duple rhythm, sombre
and expressive in sound.") (Pet 6185, 1961, 10 pp.)
5 pieces. MM, Ped. *Biog.

6.39 ENGELMANN, HANS ULRICH. Klavier Suite, No. 2,
Op. 8 (1951-52).
Gently colored music of some harmonic originality.

Common triads used with suggestions of polyharmony;
groups of tones are repeated. Rhythmic interest includes changing meters and traditional patterns.   II is
a graceful Allegretto, with markings like leggiero,
cantabile, and dolce. Traditional 6/8 rhythms. Both
tertial and quartal harmonies; some parallel triad motion. Tango rhythms appealing in Lento III. Rythmic
contrasts include triplets in a ground bass. Centered
on D, although all but one of the twelve tones are
heard in last chord; ostinato of five tones has D for
lowest tone. Presto VI is very effective movement,
lively with jazz influences--boogie bass, rough accents,
and ostinatos. Fertile with ideas. Active LH includes
extensions. (AS, 1964, 14 pp.) 6 movements, 10
min. Some Fngr. 6, some 5 & 7.

6.40 FIALA, GEORGE. Trois Bagatelles, Op. 6.
Three Bagatelles show fine craftsmanship. Tonal harmonies include traditional freely changing modulations.
Full textures skillfully attained. First Bagatelle also
printed in Royal Conservatory of Music Grade V Pianoforte Examination, published by Harris. Like the
first Larghetto, Andantino is pastel in coloring.
Broken seventh chords covering tenth range in LH acc.
Primitive, driving Allegro con fuoco acc has both repeated percussive cluster chords and treble chromatic
counter line. (GVT--assigned to Chanteclair Music--
1968, 3 pp.) Fngr, MM, Ped. 6, some 5.

6.41 FINE, IRVING. Homage à Mozart.
Admirably skillful and refined neo-classic Allegretto.
Composed of theme, three decidedly changed variations, and coda. RH sixteenths in variations create
exquisite dissonances. (B&H, 1957, 2 pp.) MM.

6.42 FLEMING, ROBERT. Ballerina.
Charming and gentle neo-romantic music. Piquant
non-harmonic tones used with traditional harmonic background. Arpeggios in each hand. Faster RH melody
includes mixtures of small and large intervals. LH
has double notes requiring extensions. Publication
conveniently printed so that three pages are spread out
at one time. (McK, 1968, 4 pp.) MM, Ped.

6.43 FORTNER, WOLFGANG. Elegy I.
Deeply felt twelve-tone work. Varied repetitions of
motives and repetitions with set transformation provide

unity. Material reappears with reversed hands.
Many harmonic seconds, sevenths, and ninths, as well
as thirds, octaves, and triads. Each hand has numerous double notes. (From 7 Elegies pub by Schott,
1951.) (In 4.9, 2 pp.) Some Fngr.

6.44 FRICKER, P. RACINE. Four Sonnets for Piano.
Inherently musical. Twelve-tone works are mostly
lyrical, gentle, and slow. Unordered set segments
used. Rhythmically fluent and uncomplicated. Gestures in III are of short duration. Surprising number
of harmonic thirds and sixths. Alternation between
6/8 and 2/4, also between legato and staccato. In IV,
marked "quiet and serene," recurring octave-domi-
nated motive alternates with flexible accelerating melody which has prominent thirds. (In 6.1, 4 pp.)

6.45 FRICKER, P. RACINE. Fourteen Aubades (1958).
Lovely short pieces of distinct character. Aubade
means morning music, or a kind of musical idyll--
most works are lyric. Idiomatic keyboard explorations in homophonic texture. Clearly tonal, while
freely using all twelve tones. In varied and unified
Andante con amore II acc has extensions in both hands.
Fast and ff Giojoso III has much rhythmic interest:
LH stabbing chordal acc divides 2/2 meter by three,
three, and two, while RH may be divided normally or
displaced like LH. Develops strong RH fingers.
Flexibly canonic Pomposo V is convincing. Exclusively octaves, with some skips. Dissonant full chords
protest strongly in the solemn VIII. Accompanying descending scales of changing colors hold together the
rubato X. LH has extended broken chords. XI, a
waltz, is delightfully capricious. While RH melody
flows along spontaneously, acc soon breaks off broken
chord extensions to join RH in two-beat slur patterns.
Acc then changes to staccato counter melody, and ends
by providing harmonic interest for RH single broken
chord reiterations. (Scho 10805, 1963, 10 pp.) MM.
6, some 5 & 7.

6.46 GALINDO, BLAS. Siete Piezas.
Seven Pieces are essentially simple, both in expression and technique, but varied, nevertheless. First
two are modal with almost no departures; III is tonal
with very few accidentals; IV and VIII are polytonal
throughout; V is tonal, but with a twelve-tone main

melody and VI is tonal, but with much chromatic motion. Allegro I has a finely integrated naiveté. In ABA form. A uses mixed modes, treble melody dorian on d and LH lochrian and mixolydian. LH acc sometimes broken sevenths moving in parallel motion. Slower B, in phrygian, is like a lament. In coupled and two-part coupled texture. In II full-sounding chordal Lento frames a more gentle and flexible Andante. Added-note chords have prominent fourths and fifths. Logical secondary contrapuntal interest. Brilliant VII is vivo with skillful play of tones in perpetual motion. Many strong finger staccato scales coupled in fifths, thirds or sixths contrasted with legato, contrary motion. Accents and short slurs throughout. (EMM, 1955, 24 pp.) MM. 6, some 5 & 7.

6.47 GENZMER, HARALD. 3. Sonatine.
Solid and satisfying. Combines fundamental simplicity and sophistication. Jazz is most noticeable influence. Commissioned by the Radio in the American Sector of Berlin for Family Music Day, 1959. Appealing Allegro has striking ostinato bass, polyharmonies, and added-note chords. Skillful construction. Hand staccato in both hands. In C. Andante most often in two-part polyphony, both linear and with some parallel sixths. Very unified. Vigorous folk dance character in closing Molto vivace. Many parallel fifths. Musically simple and convincing. In C, with frequent lowering of third and seventh tones, showing blues influence. (ScS 5067, 1960, 9 pp.) 3 movements. MM, some Ped. 6, some 5.

6.48 GENZMER, HARALD. Studies, Vol. 2.
Play of Sound, title of last Study, could describe entire collection with its resourceful textures. Much bass register. Studies in same sense as Chopin's; expressiveness transcends the technical. Tempos alternate. Tonal, using all twelve tones. Titles also in German. Harmonies in Meditation have much double inflection. Mirror motion in staccato chord acc. Melody phrases often begin and end on fifth scale tone. Builds to intense climax. Poco allegro Rhythmic Study is light-hearted and musically simple. Meters frequently alternate between 3/4 and 7/8. Hands equally emphasized. Jagged simplicity of melody in Adagio Irish Song is reinforced by coupling (sometimes in inner voice) two octaves lower. In

Prestissimo Study (p. 22) hands alternate constantly,
either in close proximity to each other or in broken
thirds. One hand often has four-tone pattern gradually spreading out while other hand repeats process with
three tones. Pianistic Molto Presto ma sempre con
fantasia perpetual motion is technically very useful.
Coupled writing two octaves apart. Lateral skips, no
thumbs under. All dynamic levels. (Lit/Pet 5929b,
1967, 16 pp.) 10 pieces. Some MM & Ped. 6, some
7 & 8.

6.49 GERAEDTS, JAAP. Zeven Essay's.
Seven Essays are vignettes of expressive and pianistic
variety. Twelve-tone set contains five major or minor
triads, so music sounds more traditional than custom-
ary. Original order of same set used in classic
twelve-tone manner throughout. Hands equally emphasized. Printed from clear manuscript. I, marked
"placidly," is poetic. Chromatic common chords and
tonal melodic fourths in first measure. Material reversed sometimes between hands. III is fanciful, with
pomposo beginning followed by sprightly alla marcia.
Finger staccato on rapid repeated tones; also hand staccato. Rapid VI is vehement; needs strength for accented strokes and repeated chords, which build in numbers of tones and dynamics. Hands alternate for striding single lines. (Don, 1954, 11 pp.) 10 min, 54
sec. MM. 6 & 7.

6.50 GIANNINI, WALTER. Modal Variations.
Well-paced piece of musical and pianistic variety.
Theme of ingenious unity uses "first six tones of mixolydian mode starting on E-flat." Theme and harmonies freely changed. Freely associated harmonies
used. Fourths prominent throughout. Chordal masses
with modulating colors exploited in Adagio Var II. Final tonic ninth with added sixth example of harmony
used. Blitheness growing to brilliance characterizes
Var III. Octaves only, in two-voice texture. Brooding mood of IV comes from theme in bass and three-
tone treble chords, usually only one tone changing
pitch. V drives along like an energetic folk dance.
Alberti type bass. Complex harmonies give "recitativo" aspect to VI. Uninhibited "scherzando" spirit of
jazz in VII brings work to rollicking ending. Many octaves and thirds. (AME, 1951, 10 pp.) 8 min. MM.
Anal. 6 & 7.

6.51 GIANNINI, WALTER. Sonatina.
Melodious, consonant work fluently spun out. Musically and pianistically conservative. Cantabile has two
themes, each generating continuous expansions. Acc,
often chromatic, has numerous legato eighth note double
notes, many of them thirds. Chorale frequently repeats melody opening, usually in upper voice. Contra-
puntally active four and five-part harmony. Spontaneous
Dance Finale is perpetual motion con brio in predominantly two-voice texture. Splendid for equal hand emphasis. Some coupled writing in fifths. Syncopation.
In pure G mixolydian mode. (AME, 1958, 7 pp.) 3
movements. MM, some Ped. 6 & 7.

6.52 GLANVILLE-HICKS, PEGGY. Prelude for a Pensive
     Pupil.
Lovely neo-romantic music. Penseroso mood and constant acc motion like Rachmaninoff. LH acc is added-
note broken triads in parallel motion; RH melody, with
acc, also frequently moves in parallel first inversion
triads. Momentary polyharmony. Some chromatic
coloring. In C. (In 6.4, 2 pp.) MM.

6.53 GONZÁLEZ, JORGE AVILA. 24 Invenciones, Op. 8
     (Primer Cuaderno).
24 Inventions (First Collection) are twelve-tone works
sometimes using same set in different pieces. Con-
cerned with traditional values of sound and repetitions.
Fairly accessible. Securely skillful. Publication aided
by Mexican Society of Composers and Authors. II, a
Moderato grazioso, fascinatingly unified by harmonic
pedal point subject to octave transpositions. Many
gentle sevenths and ninths. IV is a full-texture Cantabile espressivo. Neo-romantic in its rubato, lyricism,
and expansiveness. LH has a rapid extended motive.
Much use of fourth chords. Allegro moderato V and
VI are closely related to each other because of invertible counterpoint and inverted pitches. IX is an Andante tranquillo of expressive dynamic and tempo
changes. "Normal" chords like octaves with thirds
emerge now and then in a glowing expressiveness. Acc
has many broken tenths. (EMM, 1964, 15 pp.) 9
pieces. Some Fngr. 6 & 7, some 5 & 8.

6.54 GREGOR, ČESTMÍR. Muzikantský Popelec.
Pieces in Musicians Carnival are successful spoofs.
Harmonic surprises are obvious; not only does the har-

mony have a planned awkwardness, but other elements
are out-of-joint. If only "correct" elements are considered, music quite traditional. Most melodies are
like folk songs. Titles in Czech and German. Melodic phrases come to an end in Vagabond Song (p 6), but
harmony remains unfinished. Motive from melody flits
haphazardly about. Second melody is ridiculously
doubled four octaves away, with a few pathetic acc
notes filling the void. In The Recital (p 8) at least the
first and last notes are right. In between why the sudden chromatic sixteenths? Why the low, thicker texture chords, the monotonous polyharmony repetitions?
Perhaps the derisive "Scaredy-Cat!" melody indicates
The Recital not to be taken seriously, anyway. Translations are Variations on a Happy Song (p 3) and Pil-
grimage Song (p 10). (Sup, 1968, 7 pp.) 4 pieces.
6, some 5 & 7.

6.55 GUARNIERI, M. CAMARGO. Ponteios, 2° Caderno.
Preludes, second volume (11-20) are pleasant idiomatic
works. Neo-romantic and mildly contemporary. Several have South American rhythms. Practice for moderate extensions. All are homophonic, with acc usually an active secondary improvisatory line. Prelude 11,
marked "sadly," has a simple lyrical treble melody.
Moderate secondary contrapuntal interest. Some emphasis on broken fourths. Numerous meter changes.
Correct final bass tone must be G. 14, marked "con-
fident," has fascinating rhythm: melody has rubato
written in the rhythms while acc is continual sixteenths.
LH may have triplet across two beats, making the mel-
ody/acc three against eight. Very chromatic. LH has
many tenths. F is loudest dynamic. Tango rhythm of
15 consistent throughout the incisive and rapid piece.
Hands continually alternate, with thumb tones of each
hand accented. Added-note and momentary color harmonies. Open sounds of fourths, fifths, and octaves.
Held bass acc tone often not on the beat. 16 is ami-
able and soft. LH melody has frequent syncopations.
Basically in two voices. RH in constant sixteenth note
ostinatolike motion, with broken thirds between fourth
and fifth fingers. 19, a salon type work, has noticeably chromatic harmony. (Ric-Ba 11211, 1956, 24
pp.) 10 pieces. MM. 6 & 7, some 5.

6.56 GUARNIERI, M. CAMARGO. Ponteios, 3° Caderno.
These Preludes, third volume (21-30), are similar to

those in second volume. (See 6.55.) Four works are
obviously South American. Four are like etudes; in
general, fast preludes are abstract play with tones,
unrelated to South American stereotype. Tonal, with
mild chromaticism. Prelude 21 has perpetual motion
with constantly changing slurs for both hands. Fine
practice for fourth and fifth fingers, leaps, and rotary
motion. Often same fingers are used for each hand
because of tightly constructed figures in contrary motion. 23 is a scintillating and original Vigoroso.
Hands are rhythmically and harmonically independent.
RH rhythm is always an eighth-note arpeggiated chord
and an eighth rest; LH has perpetual sixteenth notes
with contractions and extensions. Always polyrhythmic, with RH either 3/4 and LH 2/4 (bars end at
same time for both!) or 4/4 and 3/4. No key apparent until final chord. Syncopated tango rhythms domi-
nate 26. Marked "calmly." In ABA, with melody/acc
hands reversed in B. Texture fullness comes from
many grace notes and chords with extensions added to
accompanying counter melody. Marked "mournful,"
28 has a lovely RH thumb melody in broken chord texture. Much syncopation. While RH has steady eighth
note motion, LH may move by dotted eighths. Final
tonic chord includes added second, sixth, and minor
seventh. 30 has intense brooding expressiveness.
Carries out Sonoro direction with many extended four-
tone LH chords and RH octave reinforcements.
Treble melody frequently hovers around two tones.
(29.) (Ric-Ba 11354, 1957, 22 pp.) 10 pieces. Some
Fngr, MM. 6 & 7.

6.57 HAIEFF, ALEXEI. Notes of Thanks.
Attractive, idiomatic treatment of commercial music
and jazz. Textures are reasonably full; care needed
to subdue acc. Octaves plentiful, tenth reach helpful.
Conservative. Minsky's (New York night club) Without
Care (2) is like foot-tapping ragtime. RH is busy with
thumb melody and dotted-note acc figures; has lateral
motion. Striking coda. Pleasant, lyrical Echo Berceuse is in 6/8 meter, with constant quarter and
eighth note motion--difficult to accent properly. Soprano and tenor have simultaneous motion in four-part
harmony. Gentle clash of dissonances, some of them
double inflections on weaker beats. Irresistible Little
Finale (6) is an Alla breve vivace with difficult syncopation. Many rests on main beats and elsewhere.

Chromatic. (Chap, 1961, 14 pp.) 6 pieces. Some
Ped. 6 & 7, some 8.

6.58 HAJDU, MIHÁLY. 5 Zongoradarab (1955).
5 Piano Pieces have immediate appeal of simple brilliance or lyricism. Influences from east European
dances and jazz. Frequent semi-ostinato elements.
Three longer numbers are fast. Numerous brisk octaves, first inversion triads, and thirds using forearm
or hand staccato. Lateral skips present. Strength
and endurance developed. Often modal. Thirds of
chords frequently omitted; cluster elements present.
Conservative. Titles also in English and German.
Meditation is an unassuming lyrical number of fine
unity in ABA form. Characteristic of A is coupled
writing against an upper pedal, pushed off by minor
second clash. B has legato parallel seventh chords
contrasting with treble range two-voice writing. Toccata has traditional bravura. Main melody, enticingly
syncopated, has surprising lyrical qualities. Begins
with melody in dorian mode on d, while acc is incon-
sistent with lowered second and raised fourth degrees;
last page purely dorian for both melody and acc.
Broken octaves present. Equal hand emphasis. (EMB,
1966, 22 pp.) Some Fngr. 6 & 7.

6.59 HAJDU, MIHÁLY. Szonatina (1962).
Consistent direct expressiveness characteristic of prim-
itivism. Provides healthy energetic outlet with no musical complications. Simple construction wonderfully
unified. Much non-legato touch. Tonal harmonies frequently made more percussive by added-note chords.
Allegro martellato in a has repeated harmonic second
or third acc associated with first idea and throughout
entire development section. Parallel thirds and fourth
chords. Stepwise motion usually. Interestingly textured Tranquillo molto uses three staves, outer ones
with no key signature and middle treble one with five
flats; predominant key is C. Pp coloring of figures
half a tone apart. Predominant motion by major seconds or fourths. Vivace uses lydian mode in a four-
note ostinato. Fourths alternate between hands. Equal
hand emphasis, with exercise for fourth and fifth fingers. (EMB, 1964, 12 pp.) 3 movements. Some
MM. 6 & 7.

36   Contemporary Piano Music

6.60 HALFFTER, RODOLFO. Once Bagatelas, Op. 19.
Eleven Bagatelles have elegant rhythmic and harmonic
taste. Complex enough to be pleasantly sophisticated,
no more. Modal or tonal. Frequent cross slurring;
also meter changes. Textures balanced between homophony and polyphony. Usually lyrical. Fairly traditional pianistic requirements. In IV, double inflections
of third, fourth, and seventh scale degrees give piquant effects. Attractive VI has accents and slurring
counter to the beat. Basically G mixolydian mode, but
also much else. Contrary motion in chords brings
striking dissonances. Tightly constructed V reminiscent of Bartók in its mirror writing and melodic motion restricted to seconds. IX sounds like a lament.
Folklike melody is strikingly set with major sevenths
and modal harmonies. XI sparkles with arpeggios and
other quick lateral changes; also has moderate extensions. Alluring Spanish middle section. (UME 19822,
1962, 22 pp.) MM. 6, some 5 & 7.

6.61 HAMILTON, IAIN. Three Pieces for Piano, Op. 30.
Have breath-taking touches of beauty. Masterful
changes of pace. Twelve-tone music which sounds
more traditional than usual: pitch range is moderate
and rhythms, while varied, are uncomplicated. Fluently pianistic, with hands equally emphasized. Puckish Allegro is like a scherzo; lyric melodies also appear. Repeated motives and attractive articulations.
LH has hand staccato. Main material of nocturnelike
Lento has middle range melody, harmonized in sevenths
and by LH broken line moving above and below the melody. Preceded and followed by complex chords. Final
Vivo returns to lighthearted nature of the Allegro. (In
6.1, 6 pp.) 6, some 7.

6.62 HELM, EVERETT. New Horizons.
Collection aims to summarize music in the modern idiom through Webern. Because of composer's splendid
notes, both about composing process and pianistic problems, a person acquainted only with "the works of
Bach, Mozart, Chopin, Brahms, and Debussy" will
have excellent illustrated introduction to modern writing. Helm states in the foreword that "...the object
of this book is not strictly pedagogical." Even a single
work is worth the modest purchase price. (No com-
ment about individual pieces because of composer's
complete notes.) (GS, 1964, 29 pp.) 12 pieces. MM.
*Anal. 6 & 7.

6.63 HØFFDING, FINN. Tre Stykker for Klaver.
Three Pieces for Piano have ease and spontaneity.
Neo-classic. Fast finger passages in black-white key
explorations. Varied articulations. Centered on A.
I, a delightful Allegro moderato, uses all twelve tones
quite freely. Both hands of the two-voice texture par-
ticipate equally in the lively motion. Tranquillo II has
a dolce, legato RH melody. Accurate releases require
LH finger independence. Dorian tinge. III is like I
in bright mood and exercise for RH. (In 6.6, 5 pp.)
Fngr, MM. Biog. 6, some 5.

6.64 HÖLLER, KARL. Tessiner-Klavierbuch, Op. 57.
Works in Piano Book from the Tessiner (area in south-
ern Switzerland) have charming post-romantic harmonies. Tonal, freely using all twelve tones--fine practice for reading accidentals. Homophonic writing is resourceful although traditional. A few directions in
German. Lovely and generally soft Scherzoso has fast
dance motion in spare texture. Agile articulations.
Broken RH sixths and LH tenths. Hand staccato.
Facile harmonic shifts. Some quartal harmony. Etude
is vivacious play on rapid broken triads in RH, occasionally alternating hands. Wide range. Sounds more
difficult than it is. Kaleidoscopic colors, such as closing flourish on triads of d, F-sharp, G, e-flat and
back again to d. The Bells of Capriasca (a town)
grow louder and then softer, as if one were approach-
ing and leaving the bell tower. Overtones of silently
depressed bass chord are first activated; then fuller
texture of broken chords and ninth reaches. Dance (p
20), marked Vivace and accented, has rugged strength.
Much polyharmony, as well as short spans of rapid
forearm staccato chords, particularly triads. (ScS
4750, 1962, 23 pp.) 9 pieces. 20 min, 35 sec.
Some Ped. 6 & 7.

6.65 HOLMBOE, VAGN. Klaver-Skitser (1934).
Three Piano Sketches are superior works of fantasy.
National Danish traits apparent. Treble melody of
Allegro I has remarkable variety within unity; short
fast-note passages. In e-flat. Macabre mood in Andante II, partially from downward leaping grace notes
of a seventh. In b-flat. Splendid hand staccato practice for both hands in Allegro scherzando III. Numerous printing errors in II and III should be correctable
without trouble. (In 6.6, 4 pp.) Some Fngr. Biog.
6, some 5.

6.66 HOVHANESS, ALAN. Achtamar.
An exotic but musically simple composition in two
movements, written in bass range. (Title translation
not known.) Repeated tones. I is a plaintive Adagio,
"imitating the tmpoog," an instrument. Major mode
with lowered sixth. RH melody, with no phrase repetitions, has passages of five through eleven tones per
beat. LH with much repetition on dominant, uses only first, fourth, fifth and sixth tones in disconnected
rhythms. II, an Allegro, is one-line music in two sections. First section in mixolydian mode, second more
varied. In second section hands alternate constantly
and confusingly, RH having a drone repeated acc "imitating the kanoon and oud," (Turkish zither and lute).
(Peer, 1953, 7 pp.) 2 movements.

6.67 HOVHANESS, ALAN. Allegro on a Pakistan Lute Tune,
        Op. 104, No. 6 (1952).
Hypnotic appeal. Contains both exotic and traditional
contemporary practices. Melody begins in dorian mode
and is doubled more than an octave away by octave and
fifth, sometimes by sixth and fourth. There is also
imitation. Sometimes bitonality. Melody rhythm, usually in 6/8, often ends on second eighth; also in 3/4.
In perpetual motion, with acc in smaller print. (In
6.4, 4 pp.) MM.

6.68 HOVHANESS, ALAN. Artinis.
Consistent exotic atmosphere in perpetual motion, one-
line music. Artinis is the Sun God of the Urardŭ, "a
pre-Armenian civilization around 800 B.C." First two
movements are entirely in bass range; last is first all-
bass, then all-treble. Last two movements are moderately fast; first and last have very few black keys.
First flutelike movement is "peaceful, solemn and ma-
jestic," with repeated sixteenth note motion in groups
of four; also has uneven groups of thirty-second notes.
Infrequent bass of two thirty-seconds. Last movement
has fascinating mixture of repeated and scale tones,
damper pedal blending many measures together. (Pet
6640b, 1968, 12 pp.) 3 movements. 5 min. Some
MM, Ped.

6.69 HOVHANESS, ALAN. Farewell to the Mountains, Op.
        55, No. 2.
Melodically fascinating. One-line music, usually in
constant sixteenth note motion. Considerable unity.

Marked "rapid, like an Oud (lute)." Second section
with color in treble and bass quick alternations.
Rhythmic plan of 23/16 plus 24/16 is challenging because hands alternate irregularly. (Pet 6573b, 1968,
3 pp.)

6.70 HOVHANESS, ALAN. Sonata, Op. 145.
Remarkably pure and simple concept. Neo-classic.
Often in two-voice texture, LH accompanying. Uses
phrygian and mixolydian modes with a minimum of
black keys. Includes perceptive general comments
about composer's music. Allegro is comfortable, fluent, and happy. Clear sonata form. Fairly wide keyboard range. Mystical atmosphere in Andante contrasts sharply. Alternates between polychordal arpeggios and melody with raised second degree accompanied
by cluster chords. Presto is like Allegro in form and
character. LH acc uses several ostinato patterns.
Frequently one line only. (Pet 6290, 1962, 14 pp.)
3 movements. 9 min. MM. *Anal. 6, some 5.

6.71 HOVHANESS, ALAN. Two Ghazals, Op. 36.
Exotic "misterioso" mood maintained with fine consistency. Ghazal is a composition constructed on an
"Arabic melody characterized by the frequent recurrence of a short theme." I repeats after II. I has
LH agile, pp broken-chord acc requiring constant extension and contraction. Based on a pentatonic scale.
II has chord clusters and melody harmonized by major
sevenths. (Pet 6485, 1968, 5 pp.) 4 min. Ped. 6
& 7.

6.72 HOVHANESS, ALAN. Vanadour, Op. 55, No. 1.
Luxuriant melodic and rhythmic fantasy. Vanadour is
"the Armenian god of hospitality." Music "imitates
the oud, or lute." Medium wide range, one line on-
ly--all melody. In addition to numerous unevenly
placed rests, beat is divided erratically by two through
eight equal tones. Ends with irregular succession of
3/16 and 2/16. In G lydian mode. (Pet 6573a, 1968,
5 pp.)

6.73 HOVHANESS, ALAN. Visionary Landscapes, Op. 214.
Exotic but uncomplicated. Sonorities constantly re-
newed through perpetual motion, often with repeated
tones in acc. Smooth alternation between hands required. Unusual scales. Fascinating soft resonances

in I with pedal always held. II is rhapsodic. Melody
tones always twice faster than acc pattern of eight repeated tones in same register. Frequent rests, after
pedal blurring. In V, Midnight Bell, "play inside the
piano with the fingers on the strings," is easily
learned; evocative results. (Pet 66018, 1967, 12 pp.)
5 pieces. MM, Ped. 6 & 7, some 5.

6.74 HOVLAND, EGIL. Scherzo, Op. 29, No. 1.
Charming and lightly entertaining; rather sleight-of-
hand, with double inflections, enharmonic changes,
polyharmonies, and measures short a beat. Main idea
usually in treble registers with piquant harmonies which
may move by seconds or fourths. Secondary idea includes sturdy minor seconds, fifths, and octaves in
medium to low register. Musically simple. (Ly 369,
1958, 3 pp.) MM.

6.75 HUZELLA, ELEK. Cambiate per Pianoforte (1965).
Cambiatas for Piano are serious pieces with individuality. Performer will need to seek out the expressive
intent. Titles are Invocation, Exclamation and Wail:
each moves attacca to the next. To depict the general idea of Changing, as indicated by title Cambiata,
Invocation has bass progression of harmonic major second, minor third, major third to perfect fourth, or
the reverse. Treble is often in canon with bass. In
Wail, treble imitates bass (pitch only) a tone later.
Invocation and Wail have legato double notes only.
(EMB, 1968, 4 pp.) 3 pieces. 4 min, 30 sec.

6.76 ITŌ, R. Rokudan.
Splendid variety with concentrated material. Arranger's
material is so integrated that folk melody impossible
to isolate. Rokudan is the "name of a form with six
sections," with basic material common to each section.
One prevalent descending four-note motive. Tempos
of sections (only four here) increase from Adagio espressivo to Allegro vivace. In noticeably pure pentatonic mode with two half steps; slight dorian contrasts.
Texture may thin to two parts. Many register changes;
last section adds variable dynamics. (In 6.3, 8 pp.)

6.77 JELINEK, HANNS. Suite in E, Op. 15, No. 5 (1947,
         1949).
Charming work, showing a sophisticated blend of impressionism and the Baroque suite. Many skillful

pianistic details. Combined tonality and twelve-tone
writing "in which the forms of line alternate with one
another in free succession." Traditional composition
techniques and textures. Moderato Praeludium has
bits of melody amid washes of color from broken
chords. Melody tones emerge irregularly in either
bass or treble from constantly flowing sixteenths.
Courante is a witty Vivace in the usual two-part form,
with the second half an inversion of first half. Wide-
striding staccato melody is both above and below repeated-tone acc. Excellent practice for swift alternation between hands and for repeated thumb tones in
each hand. Siciliano has sensitive harmonies changing
in manner of Chopin's e minor Prelude. To vary mel-
ody-acc pattern, there are parallel fourth impressionistic measures. Gentle Epilog (dedicated to Debussy)
has brief ideas left unfinished, luscious blend of seconds, thirds, and octaves up and down the keyboard,
and other parallel motion. (UE 12024, 1951, 17 pp.)
9 movements. 18 min. Some MM. 6 & 7, some 5.

6.78 JENEY, ZOLTÁN. 5 Piano Pieces.
Communicative atonal or non-atonal music. Quite
homophonic. Many harmonic major sevenths and some
minor seconds. Title also in Hungarian and German.
Atonal I, an Allegro molto, ben ritmico, has savage
near-cluster chords in irregular rhythmic groupings.
First two chords appear frequently, as well as a later
one of a tritone and perfect fourth. Many rests. II
is in minuet tempo. Non-tonal; G and e triads appear.
III sounds like a nocturne. Original V, Epilogo, suggests improvisatory night club music because of highly
ornate melody. Atonal work with gentle coloring from
dissonant major seventh, minor second near-ostinato
acc. Ending acc has atmospheric broken chords. (EMB,
1968, 8 pp.) 6 & 7, some 5.

6.79 JOHANSON, SVEN-ERIC. Variationer över ett Folk-
visetema (1962).
Skillful Variations on a Swedish Popular Song have much
polyharmony. Usually polyphonic. Variation 1 is quite
canonic and 2 combines 2/4 and 6/8. 3 has parallel
fifths. Inactive 4 interestingly seems to dissolve all
that came earlier. (In 5.5, 2 pp.) MM.

6.80 KARKOFF, MAURICE. Meditation, (1962).
Brooding "tender, visionary Andante." Directions like

"molto sustenuto ed elegiaco," "espressivo," and
"cantabile" indicate lyrical nature.   Fine tone study.
Recurrence of three-note motive gives some unity to
unclassified harmonies.   (In 5.5, 2 pp.)   MM.

6.81   KASANDJIEV, VASIL.   Nightmare and The Jolly Spar-
        row.
        Economical use of tones in Lento tempo masterfully
        creates Nightmare mood.   Atonal and expressionistic.
        Much rhythmic variety, most difficult a triplet across
        four beats.   The Jolly Sparrow is jovial, witty Allegro
        giocoso with meter changes in every measure!   Re-
        peated major seconds portray playful bird, in part.
        Many fourths.   (In 6.2, 1 p & 2 pp.)   Ped.   *Biog.

6.82   KAY, ULYSSES.   Four Inventions.
        Discerning neo-baroque works of distinct character.
        Lines are always musical before being pianistic; re-
        quire resourceful fingering and short pedals for legato.
        Wide stretch helpful.   Three works have subject imi-
        tation in two or three voices.   Tonal, freely using all
        twelve tones.   I is a lovely three-voice Andante mod-
        erato concentrating on a wide-ranging subject; has epi-
        sode with syncopated rhythm.   II is a delightful Scher-
        zando in 5/8 with dynamic and articulation variety.
        Frequent lateral staccato shifts.   (Du, 1964, 9 pp.)
        Fngr, MM, some Ped.   6 & 7.

6.83   KENNAN, KENT.   2 Preludes (1951).
        Virile and expressive.   While freely using all twelve
        tones, tonal because of clear bass indications.   Neo-
        romantic nature of I is indicated by direction "rather
        freely; with a feeling of yearning and unrest."   Has
        chromaticism.   Richly melodic, with one motive re-
        peated frequently.   Massive and vigorous II has basi-
        cally two-part linear counterpoint with parts coupled by
        octaves, fifths, and fourths; often in a low range.
        Much stepwise progression and contrary motion.   (In
        6.4, 5 pp.)   MM, some Ped.   6 & 8.

6.84   KETTING, OTTO.   Komposition mit zwölf Tönen (1956).
        Compositions with Twelve Tones are warmly expressive,
        related to traditional music because of octave doublings.
        Some feeling of tonality, particularly at cadences.   All
        use one untransposed tone set.   II uses retrograde
        transformation, III and VI the inversion, and IV retro-
        grade of the inversion.   Legato fingering throughout.

Andante I is in traditional texture of melody and contra-
puntally activated acc. RH has numerous double and
triple notes. Strong climax. Tranquillo V is in three-
voice imitative counterpoint. Many subject entries,
usually fourth or fifth from preceding entry. Ends
with subject doubled by octave. VI, a very expressive Poco adagio, is only number to shift meters; also has more varied beat subdivisions. VII repeats II,
and adds a ground bass of tone set to end collection
with brilliance. (Don, 1957, 8 pp.) 7 pieces. MM.
6 & 7.

6.85 KETTING, OTTO. Sonatina No. 1 (1956).
Quietly expressive and essentially simple lyric work.
Ranges and rhythms more traditional than for usual
twelve-tone work. Three movements end as if in D-
flat. One set throughout, Andante using the original
order, Lento the retrograde, Adagio the inversion,
and Moderato the retrograde of the inversion. Moderato quotes from the Andante and includes spirit of
other two. Mostly homophonic, although with secondary voices. Fluid motion throughout. Andante has a
rising first motive heard in soprano or bass. Last
few measures truly inspired. Impressive bass in the
Lento is always in octaves and rivals melody in importance. (Don, 1957, 3 pp.) 4 movements. 6,
some 7.

6.86 KIM, EARL. Two Bagatelles (1950, 1948).
Lovely and original contemporary music, expressively
simple although subtle. Modernism indicated by such
details as wide leaps and importance of single tone in
rhythmically exact place. Atonal. Dynamics never
above f, usually softer. Both numbers have many seconds, sevenths, and ninths often used hands together in
trill-like passages in the Allegretto scherzando I. (In
6.4, 2 pp. & 1 p.) MM. 6 & 7.

6.87 KLOTZMAN, DOROTHY HILL. Sonatine.
Effective, skillful neo-classic work. Tonal, with all
twelve tones freely used. Usually in two and three-
voice texture, one voice leading. Melodies of both
Allegretto and Andante have convincing line. Extrovert Allegro, in non-legato coupled writing, useful for
black key exploration in angular successions. (Merc,
1965, 4 pp.) 3 movements. MM. 6, some 5.

6.88 KÖLZ, ERNST. Emotion.
Smoothly impersonal as a machine; intricate in a self-
evident way. Pure study in repetitive sonorities. Title
may be satirical. All twelve tones revealed gradually
two at a time; music stretched out by repetitions of
harmonic tritones, augmented octaves, minor seconds,
and major sevenths. No melody, only double-note
clangs in all registers. Rapid short patterns use
dotted quarters through sixteenths. Precise pedaling
and dynamics. (UE 12404, 1955, 3 pp.) MM, Ped.

6.89 KOYAMA, K. Kappore and Yakkosan.
Both alive with 6/8 rollicking rhythms. Musically
simple Kappore has much melodic syncopation antici-
pating beat; also short portion in 2/2 and beat divided
by four in the 6/8. Rhythmical LH acc consists of
irregular drumlike jabs, either repeated bass open
fifths or middle or high range cluster chords. Gleeful
Yakkosan (a funny character) includes surprising octave
displacements as one element of the melodic fantasy.
LH acc of amazing rhythmic variety has but one four-
tone chord with second and fourth replacing the third.
Ends in rhythmic extravaganza. (In 6.3, 8 pp. & 6
pp.) MM.

6.90 KRACKE, HANS. Sonatina.
Sturdy German influences apparent in this zestful,
Hindemithian type work. Tonal harmonies use many
fourths and fifths; some polyharmony. Two-voice linear counterpoint has incidental imitation. Each hand
equally agile. Irregularly placed accents and gusto.
Opening Allegretto has flexible texture of melody and
varied chordal acc, or two-voice writing with varying
relationships. Form clarified at ending by thinning
material. Scherzino is simple and direct. In two
voices with RH melody in C; LH parallel broken
chords complete polyharmonies. (Noet, 1960, 6 pp.)
4 movements. Fngr. 6, some 4.

6.91 KÜRKTSCHIJSKI, KRASSIMIR. Elegy.
Haunting sound. Augmented second important in mode
like major but with lowered sixth. In striking texture
melody is doubled two octaves lower and the two-part
acc in the middle is divided between hands. Later,
melody is repeated and doubled a fourth lower. (In
6.2, 3 pp.) Some Ped. *Biog.

6.92 LACERDA, OSVALDO. Brasiliana No. 3 (1967).
Popular South American elements avoid the common-
place. Fine extensive foreword and analyses in Portu-
guese. Suite is designed to give performer some aspects of Brazilian music. Cururú (not translatable) of
Indian-American origin is a round dance of religious
orientation. Theme and four variations for LH alone.
Theme stated most completely in fourth variation; here
RH taps out familiar rhythms on wood of piano. Variations quite different from each other. Many thirds.
Spontaneous Rancheira (not translatable) is rapid dance
derived from mazurka; much melodic and harmonic fantasy. Basically romantic harmonies. B-flat tonic chord
preceded by B chord accompanying a B-flat scale suggests chromaticisms. Much articulation variety. III
is translated Lullaby. (IVi, 1967, 8 pp.) 4 movements. MM, Ped. *Anal. 6, some 5 & 7.

6.93 LARSSON, LARS-ERIK. Sång utan Ord (1962).
Lovely Song without Words uses LH acc of low octaves
and higher chords--splendid for practice in not looking
at keyboard. Fine tone study on melody alone in treble.
Ends in C, but otherwise all twelve tones freely used
and harmonies not settled. Much cross relation. (In
5.5, 1 p.) MM.

6.94 LARSSON, LARS-ERIK. Sonatin No. 3, Op. 41 (1950).
Appealing work confidently combines jazz and neo-classicism. Movements unified by use of same material.
Tonal, freely using all twelve tones. Fluent piano
writing. Agile Allegro has motor motion of much variety with changing meters. Often in coupled and two-
part coupled texture using a wide range. Lyrical,
blueslike Andante is expressive with double inflections
of third scale tone and other chromaticisms. Meter is
7/8, form is ABA. Three types of material in final
Allegro: bravura beginning and ending, rapid hand alternations, and lyrical section with many appoggiaturas. LH ostinato acc with extensions. (In 6.5, 7
pp.) 3 movements. MM. Biog. 6, 7 & 8.

6.95 LEES, BENJAMIN. Six Ornamental Etudes (1957).
Striking, well-constructed works. Sometimes oriental
sounding because of short-note arabesques and augmented intervals. Ostinato or a few tones or intervals
are usually emphasized in each piece. Tonal, with
very free use of all twelve tones. Frequent coupled

writing, octaves, and arpeggios. Two works in quintuple meter in a declamatory style. Commanding II
shifts between a quasi recitative largo combined with
scherzando measures and a main Andante section.
Andante has slow repeated tones alternating with fast
irregular interruptions, both coupled. Moderato III
begins and ends in a section of ornate melody with ostinato acc; acc has two-beat pattern of harmonic seventh and second. Middle section is repetitive, chant-
like, and exotic. Gamelan sounds in Allegro IV come
from acc of rapidly alternating thumb-tones a major
second apart; long held pedals also blend in more important tones, darting above and below the acc. (B&H,
1962, 23 pp.) MM, some Ped. 6, 7 & 8.

6.96 LIDHOLM, INGVAR. Klavierstück 1949.
Adagio Piano Piece 1949 has strong, unflinching character. Twelve-tone influenced. Fine combination of
dissonant chordal and rhapsodic one-line writing.
Much rhythmic variety. No particular pianistic difficulties. (Nord, 1961--also in 6.6, 2 pp.) MM, some
Ped. Biog.

6.97 LIDHOLM, INGVAR. Sonatin (1950).
Striking creativity produces many strong ideas. Passionate, but at times more tranquil. Dissonant. Ninth
reach essential. Preludium is non-tonal; has parallel
fifth chords. Well-titled Burlesk, marked Allegro
molto ritmico, is dominated by three-note motive; uses
both leaps and scales; is coupled or moves in contrary
motion. Tonal and usually diatonic; also has chromatic inflections. Andante Epilog usually has unaccompa-
nied angular melody only, or seconds and tritones moving strikingly in contrary motion. Atonal. (In 6.5, 5
pp.) 3 movements. MM, some Ped. Biog. 6, some
5.

6.98 LIPSCHUTZ, LITA. Three Episodes for Piano (1953).
Skillful abstract tone play in neo-classic style. Trans-
parent music suited to a child. In two-part texture,
RH leading. Playful Presto with wide-ranging melody.
Rhythm often three, three, and two. Meditative Adagio
espressivo. Vivace has hands moving rhythmically to-
gether, often in contrary motion and interrupted by
rests. All movements in e. Winner in 1953-54 New
York Philharmonic Symphony Society Young People's
Original Composition Project. (CF, 1955, 8 pp.) 3

min, 56 sec. Ch. 6, some 5.

6.99 LLOYD, NORMAN. Episodes for Piano.
Impressive musicality and contemporary tonal harmonies. Careful secondary voice leadings. I, a serious slow work, moves with fluid lines showing mirror
influences. Motion usually moderate, although acceleration comes with faster beat or more tones per beat.
Numerous RH double notes. Rapid III, marked "whim-
sically," often has graceful coupled flexible line which
alternates with homorhythmic chordal passages. Inter-
vallic structure important in chords. V is idealized
authentic American music with spirit of common folk.
Marked "gaily," much restless energy results from
speed, from unpredictable stops and syncopations in RH
melody, and from constant motion in LH acc. (EV,
1964, 12 pp.) 5 pieces. Some MM, Ped. 6 & 7.

6.100 McCABE, JOHN. Three Impromptus.
Works of distinct profile in neo-classic vein. Clever
harmonies border on bitonality. Hands equally emphasized. Vivo has scherzolike irregularly accented melody using many fourths. Perpetual motion RH staccato
acc has added seconds filling out to clusters. Fine dynamic variety. Lento malincolico is emotional and dissonant. Slashing percussive harmonies in Allegro marcato RH has three and four tone chords. Many melodic and harmonic fourths, fifths, and octaves. (Oxf,
1963, 6 pp.) 2 min, 35 sec.

6.101 MAKINO, Y. Sado Okesa, Hakone Hachiri, Kusatsu
        Bushi and Konpirahunehune.
Skillful arrangements have more traditional Western
touches than remainder of collection in which they appear. Imaginative introductions and interludes. Three
melodies in more common pentatonic scale, although
extra tones occur, particularly in acc. In Okesa
[girl's name] from Sado, after slow introduction with
some folk tune elements, music moves quickly. Rollicking triplet ostinato acc suggests waves and keeps
LH busy. Phrase gaps filled with fragments like repeated fourth chords or brief chromatic passages. Setting for Road Over Mt. Hakone carries out the direction "sonorous" with full chords, usually without third.
RH has rapid arpeggio and repeated double note decora-
tive measures. "Ringing of bells" heard. Fine tone
study. Song of Kusatsu [a watering place] is gay, ear-

catching Scherzando. Outrageous cluster and out-of-
key chords surely "make hearts dance." Boats Guard-
ed By Sea God Konpira is brilliant and effective Vivo.
When rapid pattern of thinly accompanied folk melody
stops, there are ff novelty interruptions. Many ff octaves. (In 6.3, 3 pp, 4 pp, 2 pp & 5 pp.) MM. 6,
6, 6 & 8.

6.102 MALIPIERO, RICCARDO. Invenzioni (1949).
"Inventions, precisely for didactic reasons, are all
written according to a rigidly dodecaphonic compositional technique; that is, using a twelve-tone row in its
four fundamental forms ... without transposition."
Polyphonic texture. For the discerning. Composer
explains completely how the twelve-tone sets, different
for each piece, are used. Textures from one voice
through three voices. Usually in free counterpoint, although there is some imitation. Traditional rhythms
and melodies: only a few meter changes and no large
skips. "Although written for didactic purposes, some
of these Inventions may be played in a concert performance." Composer advises various groupings for
recital purposes. Preface and notes in Italian and English. (Zer, 1954, 20 pp.) 9 pieces. MM, Ped.
*Anal. 6 & 7.

6.103 MAMISSASCHWILI, NODAR. Prelude No. 1, Whole-
       Tone Scales.
Much variety of technical material with two contrasting
moods. Begins with legato coupled fourths in bass register. Then cadenzalike arpeggios occur, which increase in speed and dynamics, and end in parallel motion. Last half has high treble melody in 5/8 or 7/8
over seconds or fourths for acc. Whole tone scale
predominates; half steps also. (In 6.7, 2 pp.) Some
Ped. *Biog.

6.104 MARGUSTE, ANTI. The Weasel (1959).
Amusing, Vivo finger staccato study. Often coupled
writing, at compound octaves, thirds, or closer. Syncopations and irregular accents. Whole tone scale used
almost exclusively. Cadenza passage uses quick hand
alternation. Conservative. (In 6.7, 2 pp.) *Biog.

6.105 MARTINŮ, BOHUSLAV. Fenêtre sur le Jardin.
Title of Window on the Garden gives clue to pleasantries. Suave harmonies reminiscent of Ravel. Fre-

quent added-note chords.   Two pieces are ABA in
form.   Homophonic texture, each hand having two,
three, and four-tone chords.   Thoroughly pianistic;
reach of ninth and tenth used.   I is graceful Poco andante and poco vivo.   Delightful play between raised
and lowered third.   Commercial and jazz characteristics.   In Allegretto IV one bright idea after another
adds up to scherzo impression.   Spiced by mildly percussive added-note chords.   Harmony progressions may
end traditionally, despite free chromaticisms along the
way.   (Led, 1957, 15 pp.)   4 pieces.   6 & 7.

6.106 MEHEGAN, JOHN.   Jazz Preludes.
Composer writes in foreword that in order to minimize
the problems of jazz on a concert program he has uti-
lized "harmonic techniques more advanced than those in
conventional jazz," and presented "rhythmic resources
in such a way as to avoid the need for ingrained famili-
arity with jazz rhythmic idioms."   In Prelude 1 a rapid melody moves up and down with varied scale and
arpeggio formations.   Bass descends chromatically in
long single tones.   2, marked with "bounce," has many
· ties through the beat.   Steady downward chromatic motion, with one tone of three-tone chords repeated.   Example of chromatic harmonic fullness in 4 is final tonic major seventh chord with double inflection.   Triplets
covering two beats.   6 is mostly strident and dissonant.
LH uses only octaves, sometimes in fast scales.   RH
has many second inversion triads.   7 beautifully unified, most noticeably by three-measure walking bass
ostinato.   Prominent in treble melody is raised fourth
and lowered seventh.   Climax has RH added second
chord extending a ninth.   (Fox, 1962, 24 pp.)   12
pieces.   MM.   Biog.   6, some 5, 7 & 8.

6.107 MIGNONE, FRANCISCO.   Sonatina No. 2 (1949).
Facile and convincing.   Lyrically uncomplicated music
with enough use of all twelve tones in tonal framework
for contemporary respectability.   First movement,
marked "very simple" and "all legato," is diatonic.   In
ABA form.   A opens with widely-spaced coupled writing
and continues with two-voice texture in thirds (every
other sound a tenth); B has a rhythmically displaced
melody accompanied by parallel second inversion triads.
Witty and fanciful Allegro ma non troppo marked "with
humour" and "always without pedal."   Legato two-voice
framework (some double notes) requires flexible fingers.

Varied material fully assimilated, including rhapsody-
like disruption from previous flow for the last page.
In e-flat. (Ric-Br, 1952, 7 pp.) 2 movements.
Fngr, MM, some Ped. 6 & 8.

6.108 MIHALOVICI, MARCEL.   Quatre Pastorales, Op. 62
      (1950-51).
      Four Pastorales have elegant taste in the French man-
      ner.   Fairly accessible.   Idiomatic piano writing of en-
      gaging sound, with techniques like coupled writing used
      at climaxes.   Consistent tonal harmonic style, with
      many added-note chords.   Much motive repetition.
      Works are carefully contrasted.   I is a semplice An-
      dantino.   Melodies, alternated between hands, have flu-
      id rhythms with notes tied across the beat.   Chroma-
      ticism gives gentle coloring.   Ends on the dominant.
      IV, a brilliant Allegro, has stepwise melodies often
      blurred by held pedal.   Long melody tones filled out by
      hand-over-hand, added second chords.   (Heu, 1952, 9
      pp.) 5 min, 50 sec. MM, some Ped. 6 & 7.

6.109 MILNER, ARTHUR.   Hobgoblin.
      Delightful novelty.   Fine technical practice for speed
      and lightness.   Rapid four or five-finger runs, no thumb
      under: only easiest finger-crossing-over-thumb in
      scale passages.   Practice for smooth hand alternation
      on rapid scales.   Hand and finger staccato.   Suave
      modulations and chromaticisms.   Doubly inflected tones
      bring sting to the music.   Conservative.   Written for
      piano or harpsichord.   (Nov, 1961, 5 pp.) MM.

6.110 MOMPOU, FEDERICO.   Canción y Danza 7.
      Haunting lyrical Song and Dance, spiced with slightly
      dissonant harmonies.   Each hand usually double or
      triple notes; wide reach an advantage.   Phrasing very
      regular.   In A.   Conservative.   (Mrk, 1952, 3 pp.)
      Some MM.

6.111 MORAWETZ, OSKAR.   Scherzino (1953).
      Appealing piece has melodic and rhythmic grace.   Ar-
      ticulation variety aids spontaneity.   Neo-classic.
      Much hand independence; hands nearly equal, although
      RH leads.   Legato double notes.   Harmonically con-
      servative.   In E-flat.   (In 8.1, 2 pp.) Fngr, MM.
      Biog.

6.112 MUCZYNSKI, ROBERT. A Summer Journal, Op. 19.
Splendid pianistic flair coupled with tonal harmonic
individuality. Jazz influences. Neo-classic. Secure
technical craftsmanship. Park Scene is a happy 7/8
Allegro, its melody intriguingly developed. First
strain is ostensibly repeated, yet there are unobtrusive
changes. In addition to obvious transpositions in second strain, linear counterpoint suggesting polytonality
appears. Evocative Night Rain has a flickering melody
with major sevenths and minor ninths in a high register. Active rhythms include three-beat ostinato occurring with changing meters and motives occurring on
different beats. Uses rotary motion, hand and finger
staccato, and RH over LH. Energetic Jubilee has
much rhythmic interest provided by irregular accents
and silent beats; also motion shifts irregularly between
the hands. Melodies glisten with unpredictable leaps
of major sevenths requiring quick extensions. Swag-
gering bass has harmonic major seconds and chords of
major sevenths and minor seconds. Builds to brilliant
climax. (GS, 1966, 14 pp.) 7 pieces. MM, some
Ped. 6, 7 & 8.

6.113 NIELSEN, RICCARDO. Sonatina Perbrevis ad Usum
      Petri et Karoli Mariae.
Very short Sonatina for Peter and Carol Marie is
sunny music, richly inventive. Practically same tone
set used throughout. Set contains three triads, indicating relationship with traditional harmony. Many
meter changes precisely notated. Neo-classic. Print
is smaller than usual. In the expressive Lento, material is sometimes reversed between the hands. Last
movement, marked "flowing," moves rapidly in accented triad groupings. Considerable rhythmic interest when hands quickly alternate, or join with conflict-
ing accents. E-flat is much repeated, showing another
link with tonality. (Bong, 1954, 4 pp.) 3 movements.
Some Ped. 6 & 7, some 5.

6.114 NOËL-GALLON. Préludes, deuxième livre.
Graceful Preludes, second volume, are usually dolce,
leggiero pieces idiomatic for the pianist's fingers.
Melody is usually in the treble, with broken chords
always prominent. Chromatic tonal harmony. Traditional rhythms. In Presto Prélude in G Flat Major
(6) broken chords usually roll upward from LH to RH.
Useful for rotary motion. Constant sixteenth note mo-

tion in 2/4 meter; some four against three.   First,
fourth, and sixth sixteenths emphasized.   LH is notated with six flats, RH with no flats or sharps.   Allegretto scherzando Prélude in B Flat Major (10) is a
light, charming perpetual motion.   Rapid hand and finger staccato for both hands; some repeated tones.
Subtle scale degree changes; prominent is raised fourth.
(Bil, 1953, 16 pp.)   MM, Ped.   6 & 7, some 8.

6.115 NYSTEDT, KNUT.   Sonatina, Op. 35.
Fluent and natural.   Facile melodies, harmonic charm.
Quality of sweetness often found in Scandinavian music;
however, percussive harmonies add strength.   Respecta-
bly modern, thoroughly pianistic.   Animato playfully
covers wide pitch range.   Rotary motion for LH Alberti bass and flowing lateral motion for both hands.
Some polyharmonies and two-voice linear counterpoint
with double notes in each hand.   In E.   Graceful,
pastel Allegretto has 3/8 dotted rhythms and LH brok-
en diminished chords.   Moves attacca to Allegro ca-
priccioso, which has brilliance as well as pianistic
flair in cascading passage work and trill-like double
notes.   Develops strong fingers.   Sounds more difficult than it is.   Percussive polyharmonies.   (Norsk,
1955, 9 pp.)   3 movements.   MM, some Ped.   6,
some 7.

6.116 OSTERC, SLAVKO.   Arabesque No. 3 (1936).
Well-titled beautiful piece.   Warm chromatic harmonies are distantly tonal, although root progressions are
sometimes very normal.   Added note chords.   Melodic and harmonic sequences.   Texture varies from
coupled writing to treble melody accompanied by full
chords using up to seven tones.   Marked tranquillo and
"very free in rhythm." (In 7.2, 1 p.)   Anal.   Biog.

6.117 PACCAGNINI, ANGELO.   Recreation (1964).
Sensitive and fastidious mezzotints of moderate temper-
ament.   Dynamic level never above f, usually less.
Forms are clear with ten pieces in ABA.   Phrases often regular and repeated.   Twelve tone writing with
numerous tone repetitions.   Lyrical melodies of moderate range.   Subtitle Suite for Children does justice
to childlike moods often captured, but music is by no
means exclusively for children.   Gentle Song (p 1) (also in 8.3) is indeed that.   Graceful melody mildly
angular, although legato with fingers alone.   Staccato

acc with rests. Melody and acc colored by many sevenths. Two-measure phrases in Allegretto Refrain are always repeated. RH has melody by weaker fingers, as well as shorter note acc. Ambitions achieves character through wide-interval bass melody of short slurs ending staccato, forte dynamics, and Allegro tempo. Frequent rests on first beat. Gentle Walk (p 7) is wreathed in a down-and-up acc line. Spontaneous Let's Go There, Children (p 9) is noticeable in collection for its Energico direction. Pattern of dotted rhythm and accented jabs alternates with ppp leggero, non-legato passage. My Beautiful Lady (p 12) is teasingly poised toward some open statement, but ceases before melody is completed. Low held tones add sonority. Translations are First Doubts (p 3), Secrets (p 5), Memory of Something (p 6), Discoveries (p 11), and Tomorrow (p 14). (UE 13714, 1966, 15 pp.) 13 pieces. MM, Ped. 6, some 5.

6.118 PAPP, LAJOS. 6 Bagatell.

6 Bagatelles are at the radical edge of modernity set for this Guide. Fanciful and varied works are angular and chromatic in a technique not far removed from twelve-tone. Importance given to single tones or chords in the manner of Webern. Some common material between Bagatelles such as A-flat, sometimes together with E-flat acting like a tonic for three numbers and 6 being a longer version of 2 and quoting twelve-tone set from 5. Allegro furioso 5 stands apart from others by greater length and relation to traditional writing. Contains motivic development, ostinatolike bass, a continuous rhythm (strenuous counter accents however), and primitive drive. (EMB, 1966, 14 pp.) MM, Ped. 6 & 7, some 5 & 8.

6.119 PAPP, LAJOS. Variazioni.

Variations is a serious work of strong character. Fairly accessible. Decided dissonances and quite jagged lines--many sevenths and ninths. Linear lines are important ingredients of harmonies, as shown by contrary motion in theme; major/minor chords, parallel sevenths, and unstable cadence chord also characterize theme setting. Each variation is clearly unified and seems more related to other variations than to theme; five melodic or harmonic motives from theme are developed in the variations. Slow variations as individual as faster slashing ones. Rhythms are reasonably

traditional, although rests are important.   (EMB,
1968, 10 pp.)   MM.   Some Ped.

6.120 PENTLAND, BARBARA.   Dirge.
Deeply moving.   Excellent tone study, particularly with
chords.   Tonal, only because of important placements
and reiterations of bass e, along with minor triad
above it containing both b and b-flat.   (BMI, 1961, 2
pp.)   MM.   Ped.

6.121 PERSICHETTI, VINCENT.   Seventh Piano Sonata, Op.
40.
Attractive and innately sophisticated.   Sensible balance
between simplicity and intricacy.   Masterful handling
of contemporary tonal harmony.   Noticeable and flexible polyharmonies.   Much linear counterpoint.   Transparent texture.   Dynamics generally soft.   Neo-classic.
Lyrical, grazioso Moderato has added-note and other
complex chords; ends on widely-spaced major seventh
chord, including doubly inflected fifth.   Immediate repetition of first theme half step higher hints at presence
of tonal flexibility.   Andante is dominated by gracefully
arching melody.   Vivo is scherzolike.   Non-legato and
short slurs.   Much contrary motion.   (EV, 1963, 12
pp.)   3 movements.   7 min.   MM, some Ped.   6, 7
& 8.

6.122 PISK, PAUL A.   Nocturnal Interlude.
Work of quiet lyric and harmonic beauty.   Neo-romantic.   Broadly tonal, freely using all twelve tones.
Some emphasis on melodic and harmonic fourths.   Texture is basically homophonic but much contrapuntal interest includes texture of two imitating voices as well
as fuller effect of incidental two-voice imitation.   (In
6.4, 3 pp.)

6.123 POULENC, FRANCIS.   XIIIième Improvisation en La
Mineur.
Allegretto commodo Thirteenth Improvisation in A Min-
or is an ingratiating pastel.   Harmonies often progress
by smooth transient modulations, such as to d-flat, f
and E; practice in reading many flats and sharps of
traditional harmonies with no key signature.   Melody/
acc texture is both resonant and transparent.   RH has
melody in weaker fingers as well as broken chord acc;
LH usually extended single-note passages.   Builds to
two climaxes with RH full chords.   Beginning direction

is to "use much pedal;" at the end, to hold pedal
"without changing." Note indicates that the 13th and
14th Improvisation (see 7.75) should be played prefer-
rably as a Suite. (Sal, 1958, 4 pp.) MM.

6.124 RAUTAVAARA, EINOJUHANI. Partita, Op. 34.
Well-contrasted set of movements. Main melody of
movements has many minor thirds--or augmented seconds. Resourceful piano textures. Very broadly tonal.
I has melody embedded in fast perpetual motion and
broken quartal or tertial parallel harmonies, usually
against pedal. Rapid hand alternation. II is somber
and weighty. Melody set in parallel minor sevenths,
harmonized one time against reiterated major seventh
pedal. Rapid III shifts between 6/8, 5/8 and 4/8.
Blithe, with melodic phrases clearly separated by repeated acc tones. (Faz, 1967, 4 pp.) 3 movements.
MM, some Ped. 6, some 5.

6.125 RIDOUT, ALAN. Dance Bagatelles.
First and last are fast encore-type works. Uncomplicated (neo-primitive), brilliant pieces sound more difficult than they are. Cluster chords. Syncopations and
accents bring jauntiness to first Allegro molto. Staccato forearm strokes on harmonic fifths, sixths, and
octaves, often in high register and in contrary motion.
Vivace, still more brilliant, has many harmonic seconds and passages with one hand on black keys, other
on white. Softer middle section has cross rhythms and
ostinato of two cluster chords. (P 4.) (Aug, 1959, 6
pp.) 3 pieces. Some Ped.

6.126 RIETI, VITTORIO. Contrasts (1967).
Pianistically facile works with pleasing melodies and
ingratiating harmonies. General title well-illustrated.
Neo-romantic. Freely modulating chromatic tonal harmonies spiced with dissonances like double inflections.
Sometimes modal. Variations resembles five character
sketches, with variation form only a general framework.
Begins like an improvisation, with beat divisions from
two to seven. Fourth section flows "without dragging"
over LH acc of medium extensions. Ends with dotted-
note scherzando in 5/4. Catharine Wheel or Flighty
Person (V) has fluent perpetual motion alternating with
chordal section; first involves rapid hand alternation for
predominantly one-line flickerings up and down the keyboard. Chordal section is bitter-sweet with ninths,

elevenths, and some polychords. Many meter changes,
or steady meter with varied articulations. (Gen,
1968, 14 pp.) 5 pieces. MM, some Ped. 6 & 7,
some 5.

6.127 ROCHBERG, GEORGE. Bartokiana.
High-spirited. Much ostinato. Phrasing both clear
and irregular. Two different modes often combined.
Requires speed. ABA form. A, in high register, is
in two voices, each with fast five-finger flourishes;
B has vaulting chord strokes, often polyharmonic.
Difficulties lie in mastering change in meters (including much 5/8), irregular accents, and varying articulations. (Pr, 1957, 4 pp.) Fngr, MM. *Anal.

6.128 ROREM, NED. Barcarolles (1949).
Like Fauré, with gentle mood and suave harmony.
Neo-romantic. Lovely treble melodies, with many delightful explorations, accompanied by two and three
other voices; acc includes usual barcarolle LH broken
chords. Each piece gives practice in reading many
flats and sharps, with numerous accidentals and attractive modulations. I, marked graceful, is most
tender. RH has melody in outer fingers and usually
also an accompanying voice. Gentle II, headed by ex-
cerpt from Yeats, has singing melody in four-voice
chordal setting; tones added at climaxes. III is more
"lively" with rapid treble arabesques. (HP, 1963, 9
pp.) 3 pieces. MM. *Biog. 6 & 8.

6.129 ROSENBERG, HILDING. De Kära Sekunderna (1962).
In The Lovely Second that interval is used melodically,
harmonically, and in harmonic progressions. Moderate range. Tonal, with all twelve tones freely used.
Movements played without pause. Andante cantabile
has pleasing and well-organized melody. Some familiar chords used. Poco lento artfully flits about with
much rhythmic variety. In the Allegro furioso cluster
chords and irregular stabs alternate with rapid passages in both hands, which weave in and out of
coupled writing. (In 5.5, 3 pp.) 3 movements. 6,
some 5.

6.130 SAEVERUD, HARALD. Sonatina, Op. 30, No. II.
Wonderfully skillful work, edited with great care.
"Composer's fingering." In two voices, RH leading
in first movement. Usually in treble register. In B-

flat with judicious chromaticism. Dolce Allegretto has
lovely lyricism. Fine forward motion from near-perpetual motion and sensitive chromaticism. Allegro
moderato is delightfully witty with refreshing naive appeal. Each hand has many rapid repeated tones using
finger staccato. (In 6.6, 4 pp.) 2 movements. Fngr,
some Ped. Anal, Biog.

6.131 SAEVERUD, HARALD. Sonatina, Op. 30, No. VI.
Exquisite work, with much made from little. Performers and listeners should be warned to avoid this
music if they are easily bored by extreme economy and
repetition; the real searcher will find drama in the mi-
nute changes. Care on details very beneficial to performer. In two voices. Usually in treble register.
Acc usually related to Alberti bass. In C, with prud-
ent chromaticism. Fine pedal study. Most careful
editing, with "composer's fingering." In Allegro sonata form I, first dotted idea constantly develops.
Rhythmic contrasts between dotted notes and triplets.
Opening four measures of Allegretto scherzando repeated three times with different harmonizations; pedal
for second appearance demonstrates expression changes
through its use. Much dotted rhythm, rests frequently
replacing the dot. (In 6.6, 5 pp.) 2 movements.
Fngr, Ped. Anal, Biog.

6.132 SATIE, ERIK. Cinquième Gnossienne (1889).
Fifth Gnossienne, along with other Satie works reviewed (see 4.131, 4.132, 5.123 through 5.127, 6.133,
and 6.134), were first published forty-three years after his death in 1925. It is hardly likely that these are
comparable to that master's piano works long since
published. Their musical characteristics are more conservative than others in this Guide, but since publication was delayed until 1968, they are included. Fifth
Gnossienne has lovely serenity. Balance between ornate melody and impassive chords. Half beats of melody subdivided by two through eight (excluding five);
many dotted notes. LH chords, which often move by
thirds, are in usual pattern of low root and higher triad or seventh chord; each sound always an eighth.
Many dominant seventh type chords resolve to first inversion chords on next higher scale degree. Final cadence in e, although G predominates. Form is essentially one section repeated. (Sal, 1968, 3 pp.) 3 min,
20 sec. MM.

6.133 SATIE, ERIK. Nouvelles Pièces Froides.
(See 6.132.) New Cold Pieces reveal tonal harmonic
originality, sometimes breathtakingly beautiful.
Counterpoint much in evidence amid full harmonic setting. Repeated melodic fragments, usually transposed,
invariably with a changed setting. On a Tree (II) uses
the same melody as On a Wall (I); music is faster and
acc often adds a broken chord basis. Moderately chromatic harmonies activated by secondary legato voices.
LH varying patterns use extensions. On a Bridge (III),
marked grave, begins in two voices and ends with them
inverted. Main body of work may have four voices or
full chords. Legato bass octaves. In C, but final
harmony is striking dominant ninth of the dominant with
added sixth. (Sal, 1968, 5 pp.) 3 pieces. 6 min,
40 sec. 6, some 7.

6.134 SATIE, ERIK. Première Pensée Rose + Croix (1891).
(See 6.132.) Rosicrucian First Thought has haunting
consistency. Unbarred tread of one eight-beat idea,
subtly varied or obviously transposed. Numerous two-
chord progressions tritone apart. Legato melody needs
legato fingering and sometimes skillful pedal. Melody
on weaker RH fingers, accompanied by four through
six-tone root position chords always separated by rests.
(Sal, 1968, 2 pp.) 1 min, 16 sec.

6.135 SCHIBLER, ARMIN. Esquisses de Danse, Op. 51.
Usually Allegro Dance Sketches are extrovert and ac-
cessible--not a dull moment. Often a scherzo-type
gaiety similar to Prokofieff's. Staccatos and irregular
length lines, punctuated with rests, result in much
playful energy. Small intervals and low registers frequent. Usually softer dynamics. Always pianistic,
with splendid experience for finger work in varied patterns. Tonal, with free use of all twelve tones. II
has lively rhythmic interest of changing meters, irregular accents and short exclamations. LH has acc
patterns like broken chords and forearm staccato double
notes. Some polyharmonies. Ninth reach. III has an
elfin charm with RH often trilling figures of chordal
fourths and seconds. Many sevenths in LH acc. Meter
is 5/8; frequent rests. IV is like sophisticated jazz
improvisation. RH low range, rapid passage work
gradually moves upward while dynamics change from
p to ff. Has soft chordal interlude. (AS, 1957, 14
pp.) 7 pieces. 9 min. Some Fngr, MM. 6 & 7.

6.136 SCHISKE, KARL. Etüdensuite, Op. 36 (1951).
Exuberant. Logic of mechanistic construction produces
convincing work. Unified by basic material repeated
with hands reversed, by canons and ingenious sequences. Frequent contrary motion in linear writing.
Many melodic fourths and harmonic fifths. Rapid playing predominates, particularly with scales and parallel chords. Equal hand emphasis. (Dob, 1951, 4 pp.)
3 movements. 3 min, 15 sec. Fngr, MM. 6, some
7.

6.137 SCHMIDT, Y. RUDNER. Dança Crioula (1955-65).
Creole Dance is a light novelty number. Sparks radi-
ate constantly from clash of minor seconds in conjunc-
tion with fifths, octaves, or single tones. Wisps of
melody emerge about every three measures from alternating bass-treble acc; sometimes warm, popular harmonies clothe a few melody tones. Begins Allegro,
shifts to Vivo, and then returns to last Allegro, subtitled a jongo, a fuller, more continuous version of the
beginning. "Authentic instruments" are imitated in the
jongo. Pedaling requires discretion. Direction on
page three is "jumping," on page five "with fire."
(IVi, 1968, 5 pp.)

6.138 SCHRAMM, HAROLD. Vertical Construction.
A piece like a punching bag, serving as a healthy outlet for inner tumult! More than that, a dramatic work
of angular profile, commanding authority. Some row
influences. Melodic successions of perfect and augmented fourths important element. Ostinato pattern of
harmonic major sevenths and minor ninths, etc. Flexible rhythms. Uses strong fingers. Octaves. Five
sections. (GEN, 1968, 3 pp.) Ped.

6.139 SCHUMAN, WILLIAM. Three Piano Moods: III Dynamic (1958).
Thoroughly contemporary with mechanical ostinatolike
writing. Rhythm vital and irregular. Unity and variety marvelously woven in the three sections. First
and third sections have alternation between hands; mirror writing in middle section. Dynamics in each section increase from piano to "intense forte." In mode
resembling mixolydian, but with lowered sixth and
sometimes second. (Mer, 1958, 3 pp.) Fngr, MM.
*Anal.

6.140 SHEPHERD, ARTHUR. In Modo Ostinato.
One-measure 7/4 ostinato is repeated surprising number of times, attesting to balance between variety and
unity. Tonal, with sensitive coloring. Fascinating
study in texture. Two-part writing gives way to fuller
texture which needs skillful pedaling and melody pro-
jection. Metronome mark appears too fast. (Pr,
1956, 3 pp.) MM, some Ped.

6.141 SHEPHERD, ARTHUR. Lento Amabile.
Uses wide range for beautiful blend. Very satisfying
to the discerning. (Amabile means "comfortable.")
Much LH above RH; three-stave use suggests resourceful textures. Active with secondary counterpoint. Tonal, freely using all twelve tones. (Pr, 1956, 3 pp.)
MM.

6.142 SMIT, LEO. Seven Characteristic Pieces (1949-54).
Exquisite craftsmanship with moderately contemporary
materials. Piano textures are ingenious. Quietly joyous Allegro Pastorale is graced by splendid coloring
and rhythms. Separated by rests, fragments fascinatingly begin on any one of four subdivisions of the beat.
Pedal blends predominantly high registers, with discreet support from single lower tones. Frequent rests.
In D and F-sharp. Pastorale leads attacca to humorous, brief Allegretto Arietta. Rhythm and melody are
a bewitching brew of influences from Stravinsky, South
America, and neo-classicism. LH acc usually staccato
broken chords. Jazz energy in the brilliant Ostinato.
Irresistible rhythms (syncopations, irregular accents,
and rests), tunefulness, and ingratiating harmonies.
Splendid practice for quickly changing RH traditional
chords. (BrB, 1959, 14 pp.) 9 min, 30 sec. MM,
Ped. 6 & 7, some 5.

6.143 SOMMERFELDT, ØISTEIN. Fables, Suite No. 1, Op.
10.
Masterful, almost tuneful two-voice linear counterpoint.
Effective and accessible. Equal hand emphasis. Well-
planned as a cycle. Melodic fourths and fifths in moderately wide ranges give rugged strength. Tonal, with
all twelve tones freely used. Foreword by composer in
English and Norwegian. Allegro III, characterized by
varied finger articulations, depends for contrast upon
fewer-note measures with pedal holding out enchanting
bell-like sonorities. Jolly Allegro risoluto V, marked

secco e martellato, has simultaneous slurrings for
both hands, interrupted by pedaled broken chords.
Many second and ninth stabs. (Norsk, 1967, 7 pp.)
5 movements. MM, Ped. 6, some 5.

6.144 SOMMERFELDT, ØISTEIN. Sonatine Nr. 2, Op. 4.
Spirited flow is sure and easy. Thin texture, basically two voices. Neo-classic. Polytonal influences.
Many melodic fourths and fifths. Opening optimistic
Allegro grazioso has three ideas: first uses broken
chord melody; second is more scalar, with LH acc of
staccato parallel thirds; third is quiet and lyrical.
Each idea repeated, with last changed by transposition
down a second. LH acc often fills in RH longer tones
with effective gestures. RH needs fleet fingers. Forearm staccatos. Abstract Andante semplice second
movement has two legato lines. (Norsk, 1961, 7 pp.)
3 movements. MM, some Ped. 6, some 5.

6.145 SPIES, CLAUDIO. Three Intermezzi (1954, '61, '50).
Expressive refinement with immaculate craftsmanship.
Sound is simpler than very exact notation appears;
nevertheless, sophisticated understanding needed. Resourceful pianism achieves interesting sonorities. Very
freely tonal. I has lyricism, a few marcato passages,
and much delicate wit. II is graceful. Builds to
strong climax. Top line leads, with much supporting
detail. Uses three staves. III, an Allegretto capric-
cioso, has rhythmic alertness. Finger staccato scale
lines convincing. Contrapuntal detail slips in with
ease. Extrovert and accessible. (EV, 1966, 10 pp.)
Some Fngr, MM, Ped. 6 & 7.

6.146 STARER, ROBERT. Five Caprices (1948).
Dramatically effective. Often lyrical. Fine texture
variety. Tonal, although chromatic and elusive. I is
a Moderato of two intertwining aspects: a capricious
element because of fleeting notes in varied rhythms,
and a Molto expressivo element which is melodic and
harmonic. Tenth reaches. 3 shows flexible mastery
of two-voice counterpoint. Imitation only at beginning.
At end, subject is in octaves with chordal acc. Two
convincing climaxes. Andantino 4 is in two-part form.
Each part has related lyrical melody with whimsical
staccato chords, as well as identical Meno mosso ending. Definite harmonies dissolve to vagueness. (Peer
1950, 9 pp.) 6 & 7.

6.147 STARER, ROBERT. Lullaby (1952)
Lovely lyrical work of splendid construction. Fine RH
tone study. Tonal, with added-note chords and chords
with substituted tones which often result in diminished
octaves. Chords may progress by one or more tones
changing a step. (MCA, 1954, 1 p.) *Biog.

6.148 STEVENS, HALSEY. Seventeen Piano Pieces (1933-
       1964)
Much pleasure here, although some works require study
in depth for understanding. Basically neo-classic, but
much variety. Broadly tonal. Considerable contrapuntal texture. Reach of all tenths an advantage.
Hommage à Arthur Honegger, marked calm and gentle,
is warmly expressive. Melody is in inner or lowest
voice. Short-long rhythms are found in double notes.
Andante con moto Hommage à Muzio Clementi is easy
going. Usually in two voices. Varied articulations,
with two-beat slurred figure often breaking into the
triple meter. Night Procession is a beauty. Usually
double note fourths, fifths, sevenths and ninths, except for a unifying triplet. Skillful spacings. Study in
Hemiola, marked quasi Allegretto, has fascinating variety between 6/8 and 3/4; also patterns are shifted an
eighth note later because of units of five eighth notes.
Another Waltz has lovely angular melody in one hand
or the other. While C is most important key, e is
used some; triads usually clouded by non-harmonic tone.
ABA in form, with second A transposed sometimes and
harmonization more chromatic. Invention is like a
modern Bach Invention. In two voices in D. Both subject and countersubject at times inverted. Andante con
moto From a Roman Sketchbook is expressively and
technically secure. Lone small-interval line of opening, which spreads out into wider intervals, is re-
ferred to throughout. Variety of staccato and legato
articulations. Sevenths included. Much linear counterpoint, including imitation. Finale is lightly stabbing,
extrovert, and effective; in the style of Stravinsky. Octave strokes, separated by rests, later include dissonant tones; similarly, coupled writing becomes minor
ninths. Variety in rhythmic groupings and articulations.
(West, assigned to Hel, 1968, 46 pp.) 29 min, 15 sec.
MM, some Ped. 6, some 5 & 7.

6.149 STOCKHAUSEN, KARLHEINZ. Klavierstück.
Music by leading avant-garde writer has sparse tex-

ture; at most, three tones sound together, usually only
one. Much leaping about, with a separate dynamic
mark for each tone. Rhythm quite difficult; most
troublesome measure has the normal three beats of the
very exact notation divided by two, two, and three.
(From Klavierstücke I-IV.) (In 8.3, 1 p.) Anal,
Biog.

6.150 SURINACH, CARLOS.   Three Spanish Songs and
      Dances (1950-51).
Genuine Spanish appeal and color present. Each piece
has slow Song followed by faster Dance; two Dances
end with hands in rapid, near-coupled texture. Conservative. Song I is both polyrhythmic and polymodal.
Used together are 3/8 and 3/4 meters and mixolydian
(sixth usually lowered) and double harmonic modes.
Dance I builds several times from hand staccato or
legato scales to slashing chords. Melancholy Adagio
Song III is set over open fifth pedal. Moderately ornate with fairly full texture. Allegro tranquillo Dance
III has tranquil mood plus frequent accents, octaves
culminating in ffff, 3/4 and 3/8 competing simultaneously, and strong-fingered, perpetual motion ending.
(Peer, 1953, 14 pp.) 6, some 5.

6.151 SWIRIDOW, GEORGY.   Toccatina.
Presto is useful study for arpeggios and five finger
passages in both hands. Needs strong fingers. Mechanistic perpetual motion of steady quarters in 5/4 meter; acc regularly underlines the two and three combination. In e with improvisatory harmonies. (In 6.7,
3 pp.) Fngr, Ped. *Biog.

6.152 SZÖNYI, ERZSÉBET.   Cinque Preludi.
Five Preludes are individual and varied. Mostly very
broadly tonal, although III is row-influenced. I has a
fanciful melody with brooding, chromatic ostinato bass.
II is a serious Maestoso. Severe dignity comes from
dotted rhythms, low range of bare ninths, and dissonances, including cross relations. Previous ostinato
heard as filler. V is a passionate work. Both hands
move pell mell with broken chords, arpeggios, scale
passages, repeated tones, and chord stabs. Patches
of repeated material mix with material of wider ranges.
Some feeling of polytonality with LH on black keys;
fourth chords. Short-long rhythms suggest impatience.
(EMB, 1966, 11 pp.) Some MM. 6, some 8.

6.153 TAKÁCS, JENÖ. Partita, Op. 58 (1954).
Serious, concentrated, eloquent work. Title used partially in earliest meaning of variation. Movements
three and four, or three, four, and five may be played
separately from entire work. Tonal. Introduzione, an
Andante of dignity and dynamic variety, concentrates
on repeated-note motive which returns in other movements. Texture gradually thickens. Notturno is atmospheric, with Debussy and Bartok influences. Recitativo is grandiloquent with repeated throbbings and
wide keyboard sonorities. A Canon, in essentially two
voices at the octave, is marked Andante tranquillo and
with great liberty. Brilliant Toccata Burlesca has
many repeated notes, several clearly defined sections,
and brief reminiscences of Notturno and Recitativo.
(Dob, 1958, 10 pp.) 5 movements. 11 min. MM,
Ped. 6 & 7, some 5.

6.154 TALMA, LOUISE. Pastoral Prelude (1949).
Concentrated work with ostinato tendency throughout.
Makes no concession to an easy appeal, thereby gain-
ing awesome attraction. Discriminating timbres within
controlled limitations. Each hand has as many as
three carefully written note values requiring independent fingers in extended positions up to a tenth. Exact
pedaling necessary. Tonal. May be used before composer's Alleluia. (CF, 1952, 3 pp.) 4 min, 15 sec.
MM.

6.155 TANSMAN, ALEXANDRE. Quatre Nocturnes (1952).
Four Nocturnes are gentle, neo-romantic pastels. Appeal depends upon harmony, often of polyharmony deri-
vation. At least ninth reach needed. "Accidentals are
notated separately for each hand." III unified by recurring melody ranging between perfect or augmented
fourth. Has doubly inflected common chords and parallel major sevenths. In IV, a pp Lento, moderately
rhapsodic treble melody is accompanied by two-beat
ostinato. (UE 12096, 1952, 4 pp.) 6 min. MM. 6,
some 5.

6.156 TCHEREPNIN, ALEXANDER. Expressions, Op. 81.
Clever works fertile with ideas. Apt title depictions.
Idiomatic piano writing with variety of ranges and
touches. Fine analytical foreword. Entrance is like
Stravinsky with matter-of-fact accessibility and irregu-
lar motor rhythms. Very Russian mood of The Hour

of Death is evoked by somber bass or treble chords
(often of unusual spacings within the octave) alternating
with recitativelike melody.   Witty At the Fair contains
polytonality (including wide-range chords), changing
meters, and deft pedaling.   Barcarolle is neo-romantic
and traditional.   Provides practice in subduing strong
fingers on active acc.   Mood of At Dawn aroused by
shrill bird calls and pianissimo chirps in very high
range.   Beats divided by three through seven in unmetered music.   Many rests blurred by long pedals.
(MCA, 1951, 19 pp.) 10 pieces. *Anal. 6, some
5 & 7.

6. 157 THOMSON, VIRGIL.   Portraits, Album 3 (1930-40)
Refreshingly bright and witty.   Lovely naive music
provides experience with polytonality, polyharmony,
and dissonant counterpoint; also at times unusually consonant.   Disparate elements often combined in one
work.   Very complete fingering.   For each Portrait
"the subject sits for his likeness as he would for a
painter; and the music is composed in front of him,
usually at one sitting. "   The high-spirited Toccata:
A Portrait of Mary Widney has suggestions of folk
tunes.   Cross-relations are particularly telling.   Uses
finger, hand, and forearm staccato in both hands; RH
has rapid repeated tones.   Outrageous polyharmonies
in Prelude and Fugue: A Portrait of Miss Agnes
Ringe result from imitation; cavalier treatment of
form.   Prelude begins with the fugue subject and the
Fugue is generally more homophonic than polyphonic.
Uses legato chord fingering.   The Bard: A Portrait
of Sherry Mangan starts and ends straightforwardly in
two-voice texture in E-flat with no accidentals.   Middle section is brash with f polyharmonies, including
reversion to first melodic material, but with acc in
D.   LH has full chords and fast broken chords.   Rapid Canons with Cadenza: A Portrait of Andre Ostier
has joyful flair.   In A-flat with no accidentals.   Brok-
en chords included.   Ends brilliantly in octaves.
(Merc--assigned to GS, 1950, 24 pp.) 8 pieces.   Fngr,
Ped. 6 & 7, some 5.

6. 158 THORNE, FRANCIS.   Eight Introspections (1959).
Refined craftsmanship includes uncommon number of
fine details.   Line of motion compelling.   Despite
title, half the works are outgoing.   Broadly tonal.   I
is an Allegretto of much wit.   Rhythm and articula-

tions charming with subtle variety. Many meter
changes. Usually two-voice texture. Some invertible
counterpoint. Adagio calmo V is expansively romantic,
in part because of wide-ranging, lyrical melody. Polychords. LH has many sixths, RH augmented octaves.
Fine climax. VII is beautiful. Numerous doubly inflected chords and sixths. VIII is an extrovert Presto
vivace. Alternates often between 6/8 and 3/4. Ideas
change quickly. Acc uses harmonic seconds. (II.)
(Mrk, 1965, 16 pp.) 6, some 7.

6. 159 TRAVIS, ROY. Five Preludes.
Urbane expressiveness brushed with sentiment. Knowl-
edgeable and fairly traditional piano writing. Fine variety of articulation. Tonal, with all twelve tones freely used. 2 is an Andante sostenuto, its lovely melody
often in baritone register. Resourceful homophonic texture with secondary contrapuntal interest. Chromatic
harmonies emerge now and then with warm colors. 4
is a nostalgic Barcarola. Melody often ornate. Texture is full, but also open with staccatos. 5 is an effective, almost virtuoso Con fuoco alive with bold melodies, accents, syncopations, short slurs, and staccatos.
High spirits break midway into a bass ostinato of popular origin. Full keyboard exploration. (Pr, 1966, 9
pp.) Fngr, MM, Ped. 6, some 7 & 8.

6. 160 VERRALL, JOHN. Autumn Sketches.
Refined, as well as passionate, lyricism found. Complex expression is pursued with splendid craftsmanship.
Flexible moods. Varied rhythms, with directions like
"pliable" and "rubato. " Tonal, with all twelve tones
freely used. Evening in September resembles Brahms
in its care, its varied inner phrasing, and its sonority
of sixths. Momentum is "gently moving. " Constantly
changing dynamics. Autumn Splendor demonstrated
both "with a joyous abandon, in a free style" and in
calmer passages. Freer measures are marked by im-
petuous lines climaxing with sforzandos; tranquil por-
tions have lovely harmonies anchored by repeated tones.
(VMP, 1968, 12 pp.) 5 pieces. Some Ped. 6 & 7,
some 5.

6. 161 VERRALL, JOHN. Four Pieces for Piano.
Works of splendid craftsmanship with skillful melodies.
First and last fast numbers (only one is slow) have
motivic play in the manner of Baroque music. Form

repetitions apparent but varied. Tonalities are clear
at focal points, otherwise all twelve tones freely used.
Practice for varied finger patterns, including extensions. Lament becomes overwhelming in the middle
section where texture thickens to contrary motion
thirds in each hand. Melody in treble except at cadences, where a secondary voice enters most effectively. Acc has freely associated chords and long
rests. Toccata has fluent two-part linear counterpoint;
texture changes to coupled writing for main motive or
to voices added at will. Convincing jagged lines.
Equal hand emphasis. (UWP, 1954, 9 pp.) MM. 6
& 7.

6.162 VOGEL, WLADIMIR. Nature Vivante.
Works in Living Nature are fancifully expressive. Very
pliable rhythms. Much variety of articulation. From
beginning to end of the collection the tertian harmonies
become more chromatic, with numerous added-note,
seventh, ninth, and augmented sixth chords. Wide
reach helpful. Quite Disagreeable (p 3) has brief and
highly varied whimsical spurts, separated by holds.
Grace notes and rapid chord displacements. Lush
chromatic, full chord harmonies characterize Weary
and Plaintive (p 6), as well as apt stopping and short
rests. Joyous (p 7) builds to climaxes through reiteration of patterns. Quick skips in LH and rotary motion in RH. Translations are Stanza from an Album
and Gray Prelude (p 1), and Poetic Piece (p 5).
(Hein, 1962, 7 pp.) 6 pieces. Some MM, Ped. 6 &
7, some 5.

6.163 WARD-STEINMAN, DAVID. Three Lyric Preludes.
Exquisite musical sense governs these works. Usually one very beautiful melody is present, primary or
secondary. Broadly tonal chords often the result of
voice leadings. Variable chord spacing makes wide
reach useful. Cluster chords in III grow to use "entire forearm." "These pieces are suitable for either
piano or organ," with notation indicated for each instrument. Primary aim is musical, rather than idiomatic to either instrument. Moderately fast I has
pandiatonic harmonies. One voice always moves.
Hands reversed upon return to first section Flexible
shifts from conjunct to disjunct melodic line. II, like
other numbers, requires resourceful fingering. (HiP,
1968, 10 pp.) 6 min, 5 sec. Some MM.

6.164 WELLESZ, EGON. Drei Skizzen, Op. 6 (1911).
Atonal, dissonant Three Sketches show romantic tem-
perament and often bigness of gesture. While not a
necessity, wide reach helpful. 1, marked "dreamy"
and "tender," has lovely full-texture chromatic chords;
fourth chords also. Chords move in streams. Fero-
cious 2 has some coupled writing with wide extensions.
Expressive 3, marked "defiant," varies in dynamics
from ppp to ff and in texture from two voices to eight-
tone chords. Numerous tritones and perfect fourths.
Other directions are "somewhat slower" and "ponder-
ous." (Dob, 1963, 4 pp.) MM. 6 & 7.

6.165 WELLESZ, EGON. Triptychon, Op. 98 (1966).
Three Pieces are impressive for beauty of line. I and
III are atonal. II is broadly tonal. Moderato Grazioso
I has wide range. Irregularly mixed rhythm of two
through six divisions of beat make flexible line. Single
line of numerous thirds and sevenths punctuated spas-
modically by chords. Repeated chords in middle section. Cantabile II is an accessible lyrical, Andante
semplice. Begins with two measures of coupled melody using both major and minor thirds alternating with
two chordal measures. Ends tonally. Appassionato III
is savage with dissonant ostinato chords and vaulting
lines. Middle Vivace section is thinner, even playful.
(Dob, 1967, 8 pp.) 6 & 7.

6.166 WELLESZ, EGON. Zwei Studien, Op. 29 (1921).
Two Studies are slow and gently expressive. More
immediately accessible than many works in Viennese
school. Amid very chromatic harmonies are chord
repetitions, such as "tonic" of f-sharp b-flat f in 1
and chords with a perfect and augmented fourth in both
1 and 2. 1 combines mysticism and whimsy. Repeated four consecutive scale tones, ascending or descending, in eighths or sixteenths. II has rhapsodic
passages and ostinato acc. Sometimes the two elements are joined in five against four rhythm. Rapid
lines of irregular extended intervals in each hand.
(Dob, 1963, 3 pp.) 6 & 7.

6.167 WILLIAMSON, MALCOLM. Five Preludes for Piano.
Keen musical ear guides creation of sure programmatic moods. Three slow and two faster works are re-
motely tonal. Ships, marked Adagio molto, are depicted on the foggiest of seas. Three staves used to

notate texture where very low chords alternate with
medium high, more melodic material. Pedal effectively blends very soft sounds (including octaves, fifths,
and cross relations) in an economical manner.
Theatres brashly evokes jazzy atmosphere. Syncopated single-tone broken chord melodies and fanfare
blasts, along with crisp bass triads produce one mood;
another is more sultry with soft major seconds and
minor ninths accompanied by plain chords in irregular
rhythms. Tonal harmonies ingenious. Incredible authenticity of Temples includes bell mixtures from compound chords using fourths and a third, chants with
stepwise melodies, and modal harmonies. (JW, 1966,
14 pp.) Ped. 6 & 7.

6.168 WILLIAMSON, MALCOLM. Travel Diary, New York,
        Vol. 5
Attractive short pieces which fit programmatic titles
with pleasing aptness and taste. Modernisms are
slight. Each piece technically consistent. Probably
most appealing to early teenagers, then children. In
each of the five volumes (see 4.165, 4.166, 4.167 and
5.156) last piece is first piece in reverse. Explana-
tions of titles, when needed. Present volume ideal for
teenagers needing bright and mildly brash material.
Some cluster chords. Frequent parallel motion harmonies. Subway Rush uses quick hand alternations;
RH has thirds and LH added seconds. Complex
rhythms in 5/4. Allegretto vivace Greenwich Village
has much rhythmic interest from irregular accents,
frequent rests, pedal tone in various places, and triplets stretched across two beats. Incisive percussive
polyharmonies, with RH on white and LH on black
keys. Humorous atmosphere of Central Park (Riding
School) created by outrageous polytonalities. Eight
different meters used. Tango rhythms. Hands alternate with rapid five-finger continuous passages.
(Chap 45910, 1962, 18 pp.) 6 pieces. Some Ped.
*Anal. 6, some 7.

6.169 WIRÉN, DAG. Improvisationer, Op. 35.
Improvisations are accessible. Neo-romantic. Traditional tonal harmonic materials mixed untraditional-
ly. Require pedal judgment. I is a serious Largo of
full texture, using three types of material: octave
proclamations harmonized arbitrarily by common
chords in lower register with whole tone influences,

lyrical chromatic harmonies, and faster lines. III is
a Presto with RH fast legato thirds antioipating the
beat. LH is in perpetual single-note motion with short
extensions. Influenced by mixolydian mode. Has long
crescendos from pp to ff. V is a Molto expressivo
having, like I, a blend of tonality with whole tone influence. Arabesques in melodic line sound oriental.
A measure ostinato always present. Full homophonic
texture skillfully varied. (Geh, 1960, 10 pp.) 5
pieces. MM, some Ped. 6, some 7.

6.170 ZYTOWITSCH, WLADIMIR I. Prelude No. 4 (1964)
Interestingly alternates f percussive chordal motto with
p rapid passage work; latter is often coupled by different intervals. 9/8, 2/4, 10/16, 3/4, 3/8, and 5/8
used in near-perpetual motion. In a, with added-note
chords; suggestion of polyharmony. (In 6.7, 2 pp.)
Biog.

7.1 Greek Piano Music, Contemporary, Book I, ed by
    Günther Becker.
    Five works are reviewed. (See 6.8, 7.35, 7.85, 8.64
    and 8.82.) Most are quite contemporary, including
    three twelve-tone works. Foreword and biographies in
    English and German, titles also in Greek. Contains
    pieces by Adamis, Gazouleas, Joannidis, Leotsakos,
    Papaioannou, Sicilianos and Skalkottas. (HG, 1967, 14
    pp.) 7 pieces, 7 composers. MM, some Ped. 7 and
    8, some 6.

7.2 Yugoslavian Piano Music, Contemporary, Book 2, ed
    by Rudolf Lück.
    Fine works. Often markedly contemporary. Five
    works reviewed. (See 6.116, 7.28, 7.79, 7.81 and
    8.65.) Introduction and biographies in English and Ger-
    man; Yugoslavian added for titles. Contains music by
    Devčič, Malec, Osterc, Papandopulo, Ramovš and
    Sakač. (HG, 1966, 23 pp.) 6 pieces, 6 composers.
    Some Fingr, MM, Ped. Biog.

7.3 ABSIL, JEAN. Grande Suite, Op. 62.
    Idiomatic works in which skilful play with sonorous ma-
    terials is emphasized, as in the French manner. High-
    ly chromatic tonal harmony indicated by concluding
    chords like triad with lowered fifth or a major eleventh
    chord, evidence also of harmonic conservatism of col-
    lection. Each many-noted work has near perpetual mo-
    tion, often of a broken chord nature. Vivo Scherzetto,
    ABA in form, has polyharmonies and tertial chords
    with raised root. Much varied and rapid figuration in
    each hand. The brilliant Toccata is music of substance.
    Alternating-hands technique used with much diversity.
    Frequent parallel motion. Continual meter changes,
    such as from 3/4 to 3/8. Well-spaced climaxes are
    convincingly prepared for. (SF, 1953, 22 pp.) 4 move-
    ments. Some Ped. 7 & 8.

7.4   ADLER, SAMUEL. Capriccio (1954).
      Buoyant, neo-classic music. Linear counterpoint with
      much contrary, sometimes mirror, motion; one line
      sometimes expanded to parallel moving harmonic mass,
      such as triads. Touches of polyharmony. Numerous
      meter changes in a near-perpetual motion. Forearm
      and hand staccatos. (In 6.4, 3 pp.)

7.5   ARIZAGA, RODOLFO. Sonatina, Op. 6.
      Splendid consistency. Performer acceptance depends
      to a great extent upon acknowledging augmented or di-
      minished octave as readily as usual perfect octave;
      many cross relations. Skillful transitions in the forms.
      Allegro semplice has relentless traditional long-short
      rhythms of 6/8 meter; dramatically breaks into dotted
      rhythms at the climax. Most often in two-voice tex-
      ture; LH acc has transitory countermelodies. Many
      melodic tritones. F mode may include mixolydian col-
      oring. Mood of sustained seriousness in Idilio. Study
      in slightly shifting biting sonorities: one passage has
      ascending paired octaves a second apart anchored by re-
      peated augmented octaves. Texture builds to expansive
      fullness. Allegro Quasi Toccata requires fluent finger
      work. Constant sixteenth note motion, usually LH on
      the beat and RH acc off the beat. In phrygian mode on
      a. Neo-classic middle Allegretto section is in two-
      voice staccato texture. (Ric-BA, 1961, 13 pp.) 3
      movements. MM, some Ped. 7, some 6.

7.6   AUCLERT, PIERRE. Pastorale et Gavotte.
      Gentle works of light tasteful content. Simple diatonic
      treble melodies with polyharmonies or doubly inflected
      harmonies. Pastorale sounds like a broken music box.
      Melodies move by step. Harmonies often move by
      parallel motion, with broken chords in both hands. RH
      melody with weaker fingers. Similar techniques con-
      tinue in the Gavotte. LH adds broken fourth chords.
      Ending melody in first section has phrygian coloring.
      Middle section has close-range four-tone chords alter-
      nating with lydian melody. For piano or harpsichord.
      (Bil, 1968, 9 pp.) MM.

7.7   BABADSHANJAN, ARNO. Picture No. 4, Intermezzo.
      Mildly rhapsodic, graceful work with extreme ranges.
      Strict twelve-tone technique. Except for low held tones
      and octaves for sonority, usually one-line music; ends
      in two voices with original and retrograde order used

simultaneously. Slow and fast tempos alternate; slow
tempo sections repeat some material. (In 6.7, 1-1/2
pp.) Biog.

7.8   BACON, ERNST. The Pig Town Fling.
Delightfully direct, pure, and uncomplicated Americana
--like a cakewalk. "Tingly," "with sparkle," and "hi-
lariously" describe its spirit. Syncopated treble
rhythms against a "back-and-forth" steady bass. Five
sections centered on e-flat, e-flat, G-flat and C merging into A, where piece ends softly, out of energy.
Accidentals are rare. Particular skill shown as sections gradually dissolve. RH uses finger agility, LH
forearm staccato. Each hand usually has only one tone
at a time. (In 6.4, 6 pp.) MM, some Ped.

7.9   BADINGS, HENK. Adagio Cantabile (1967).
Like a luxuriant modern Chopin nocturne. Fine RH
tone study. C-sharp tonality overlaid with garlands of
chromaticism. ABA in form. Richly homophonic texture in A has main melody in treble and much secondary contrapuntal motion. Very ornate treble melody in
B accompanied by five-tone, near-cluster, semi-ostinato chords in tango rhythms. A, when repeated, has
shorter notes than at first. Cramped appearance of
"composer's manuscript" may be irritating. (Don,
1967, 4 pp.) MM, some Ped.

7.10 BERGER, JEAN. Sonatina.
Appealing, brightly neo-classic, and witty music. Basically tonal, with flexible chromaticism and frequent
double inflections. Changing meters and varied slurring. Moderate ranges. Second movement, a tender
Andante, is lyric tone study for RH. Harmonies include incidental polyharmonies, chords without thirds,
and common chords progressing by seconds. Last Molto vivo movement is a high-spirited rondo. Composer
has facile talent for jazzy syncopation, lush parallel
motion harmonies, and touches of polyharmony. Acc
often rapid broken thirds. Equal hand emphasis. (Dit,
1952, 11 pp.) 3 movements. MM. 7, some 5.

7.11 BERKELEY, LENNOX. Concert Study in E Flat.
Pleasant, fluent Allegro vivace. Useful for equalizing
strong and weak fingers of RH in rapid four-note figures spanning a seventh or octave. Some RH arpeggios
in varied white-black key explorations. LH has inci-

dental rapid passage work. Shifts from perpetual motion are effective. Frequent melodic and harmonic
fourths. ABA in form; B is slower and has LH extensions. Flexible use of all twelve tones. (Ches, 1956,
7 pp.)

7.12 BERKELEY, LENNOX. Improvisation.
Graceful melody and tonal harmony exploration. Splendid flowing line uses more of the small-step theme
from Pantomime section of Falla's El Amor Brujo
than at first presumed. Fairly wide range and moderate extensions. A (andante) B (piu vivo) A in form;
B is like a cadenza using many double notes, particularly thirds. In e, ending with tonic seventh in bass.
(Ches, 1960, 3 pp.) MM.

7.13 BERKELEY, LENNOX. Three Mazurkas.
Neo-romantic works pay admirable "hommage to Chopin," but harmony more chromatic and modulations
more daring. Contain the charm, lyricism, and rubato traditional in mazurkas. I is spontaneous. Much
melody repetition and a few secondary melodies.
Some LH extended broken chords and RH quick passages. II is an Allegretto with natural flow. Clear
dynamic contrasts. ABA in form with subtle transitions between each section. III has full-throated brilliance with fuller texture than other numbers. LH
shifts up and down considerably, often with octaves
and three-tone chords. RH has some figuration using
moderately wide range. (Ches, 1951, 9 pp.) 8 min,
30 sec. MM. 7, some 6.

7.14 BERNSTEIN, LEONARD. Five Anniversaries (1949-
1951).
Pleasant, stylish, and facile. Show influence of Stravinsky and Copland. Tonal; C-sharp used in one
piece. Tenth reach helpful. Allegro con anima For
Lukas Foss veers fluently about among several basic
ideas: among them is a two-voice canon, a static area of sevenths and ninths with cross slurrings, and a
second canon, marked "scherzando," with octave
leaps. Meter alternates between 4/4 and 3/4 or combines them in one measure. For Elizabeth B. Ehr-
man overflows with enthusiastic jazz traits. Hand staccato bass ostinatos, treble blues notes, and percussive
harmonies play a part, as do varied articulations.
Alive with changing dynamics. Lonely For Susanna

Kyle has melody which skips about. Recapitulation is
first in E, effectively transposed from C. (AE, 1964,
11 pp.) MM. 7, some 5, 6 & 8.

7.15 BRITTEN, BENJAMIN. Night-Piece.
Lovely, fanciful work uses full keyboard range. Much
reliance on pedal to blend small-step, bell-like impressionistic mixtures. Part of the acc alternates between two tones, sometimes with octave displacements,
other times with rapid repeated tones which need pianissimo handling. High treble unmeasured arabesques
without pedal provide variety. In B-flat. Ninth reach
necessary. "Written for the Leeds International Pianoforte Competition, 1963." (B&H, 1963, 7 pp.) MM,
some Ped.

7.16 BRUBECK, DAVE. Brubeck, Vol. 1.
Original themes and improvisations transcribed by
Frank Metis from Columbia Records Album Brubeck
Plays Brubeck. Those acquainted with Brubeck jazz
need little commentary. For others there is much to
be gained: jazz rhythms, reading with full chordal
textures and many accidentals, as well as compositional procedures in the improvisations or variations.
Tenth reach necessary. Contains general note to performer. The Duke (Ellington) has first strain with
many parallel motion treble triads. Second strain uses
full polychords moving in contrary motion. In later
strain splendid climax achieved over a dominant pedal
as harmonic rhythms accelerate with full-texture chords.
Swing Bells begins with two pages of "rubato-cadenza"
--melodic fantasy over a dominant pedal--followed by
additional measures of introduction. Main material has
chromatic full-texture seventh and ninth chords. Fascinating coda uses fourth chords, revealed in final cadence as a part of the familiar added second and sixth.
Other titles are When I Was Young, Walkin' Line and
In Your Own Sweet Way. (Der, 1956, 26 pp.) 5
pieces. Biog. 7, some 6 & 8.

7.17 BRUBECK, DAVE. Brubeck, Vol. 2.
Melodies more spontaneous and harmonies frequently
less complex than Vol. 1. (See 7.16.) Some very general remarks by Brubeck. Weep No More has splendid
balance between tension and relaxation. Melodic fantasy sometimes captures attention; at other times ur-
gent harmony is focal point. Piece is Brubeck's "per-

sonal favorite...." Triple measures in The Waltz only a little more numerous than "half-time" measures.
Waltz measures include those with very simple melody
and others filled out by ascending arpeggios. Sections
in 4/4 have many full chromatic chords, including LH
tenths. In addition to normal dotted rhythms there are
short-long rhythms. (Der, 1956, 26 pp.) 4 pieces.
Anal, Biog. Some Ped.

7.18 BUSH, GEOFFREY. Sonatina.
Transparently clear, neo-classic tonal music. Amid
some clichés, lively intelligence is shown in piece's
secure propulsion. First movement, marked "moderate," combines contemporary characteristics like
coupled writing, two-part linear counterpoint, melodic
motion by fourths, and changing meters. Contrary
motion may extend to extreme ranges. In the digni-
fied Molto moderato, treble rhythmic fantasy has beats
divided by two through ten (excluding seven and nine).
LH acc has repeated throbbing slow strokes moving by
single step at long intervals. Each hand usually plays
single tones. Last Allegro has many characteristics
of a two-voice fugue, although there are long episodes.
Contrary motion and melodic fourths again prominent.
(Elk, 1966, 15 pp.) 3 movements. 8 min. 7, some
6.

7.19 CARR, EDWIN. Five Pieces for Piano.
Compelling musical impulse in effective twelve-tone
music, whether strident or dolce. Wide range, but
only moderately full texture. Ninth reach needed.
Same tone set used for all works. Collection well-
planned as a unit. Toccata, both bold and gentle,
flits about in register with fine wit. Supple rhythms
are of medium difficulty. Allegro one-movement Sonata has a surprisingly lyrical, leaping line. Chordal
stabs for acc. In recapitulation melody is heard two
octaves lower, then one octave higher. Variety provided by repeated interludes of dense chords and by
slower passage of two-note slurs. Neo-classic Allegro Finale is spontaneous and high-spirited. Fine formal integration and pacing between unity and variety.
Splendid articulation variety. Many syncopations.
Rousing climax at end with opening ostinatolike pattern
in double notes. (Ric-L, 1968, 14 pp.) MM. 7,
some 5 & 6.

7.20 COOPER, JOHN. 3 Bagatelles, Op. 13.
Both accessible and complex. Alludes to American
folk music, has Coplandlike sounds. Creative surge
evident with multiple musical ideas well assimilated.
Wide reach helpful. Edited in fine detail. Moderato
I, changing to allegro and lento, shows splendid dramatic instinct. Various cluster chord elements, as
well as fourths and fifths. II is slow and poignant.
Bell sounds. Ninth chords. III, Allegro ma non troppo, is ebullient with implied and realized joy. (B&H,
1966, 6 pp.) MM, some Ped. 7, some 6.

7.21 COULTHARD, JEAN. Devil's Dance (1953).
Hard-driving, well-constructed Allegro marcato mar-
vellously depicts title. Biting dissonances (such as
tussling between D-natural and D-flat for the tonal center), sharp staccatos, and chromatic insistence create
diabolical mood. Irresistible push toward two screech-
ing climaxes. Many single and double-note hand staccatos. (In 8.1, 2 pp.) Biog.

7.22 COULTHARD, JEAN. Etude No. IV.
Con fuoco piece of fine consistency sounding more difficult than it is. Broken polychords. RH fifth finger
strengthened. Steady RH sixteenth rhythm often contrasts with LH dotted octaves. Equal hand emphasis.
Varied textures, dynamics, and ranges. (BMI, 1954,
4 pp.)

7.23 COULTHARD, JEAN. Prelude No. 2, Torment.
Logic of construction shown in consistent use of two
types of material. First has sweep downwards in near-
coupled writing, RH being one or two pitches ahead of
LH; second has snatches of low, brooding RH melody
with LH broken chord ending on a major seventh. Concluding fifths on D-flat compete with sustained leading
tones. (BMI, 1959, 2 pp.)

7.24 COULTHARD, JEAN. Prelude No. 3, Quest.
Splendidly integrated work with convincing curve of in-
tensity. Title depicted by harmony which never fully
settles: LH broken chord acc is clear, but RH is off
a little, such as ending harmony on E, but with f triad
added. Insistent melody centered on tone a half step
away from prevailing chord also suggests title. Continuous LH tenth extensions. Polyrhythms of three
against two and four against three. (BMI, 1959, 3 pp.)
MM.

7.25 DAVIS, ALLAN. Razorback Reel.
Rough, folklike ritmico is surely an audience-pleaser.
Effective and varied pianistic requirements. Parade
of exuberant ideas prefaced by fiddler's rasps and introduction. First broken-chord tune repeated in bass
register at end of section A. Mode is prevailingly f
dorian with transitory shifts to A-flat, D-flat and f
aeolian. "Burlesque" section B is centered on F;
raised fifth prominent in acc, and again there are
transitory shifts. Repetition of A greatly varied. Will
develop finger strength in varied single note explorations, clarity in coupled writing, and quick melodic and
full chord skips. (Oxf, 1963, 5 pp.)

7.26 DELLO JOIO, NORMAN. Nocturne in E.
Lovely, relaxed number provides many pianistic oppor-
tunities. Medium wide-range treble melody, the most
prominent of four voices usually present, uses singing
tone; LH acc sometimes three and four-tone chords.
Texture needs careful pedaling and voice balancing for
clarity. Chromatic harmony. Wide reach helpful.
Some jazz influences. (CF, 1950, 3 pp.) 2 min, 20
sec.

7.27 DE MEESTER, LOUIS. Trois Nocturnes (1947)
Three Nocturnes are sensitive pieces requiring interpretative maturity. Have bars but no meters. Little
editing in easy-to-read manuscript. I is poetic and
"without rigor." Twelve-tone set and its retrograde
used many times. Sense of line necessary. Calme II
is lovely. Uses only white keys and ostinato acc of
superimposed sevenths. More accessible than I or III.
III is fluid. Ornate improvisation with many arpeggios
and trills. Many extensions. Climaxes on last page
with a polychord of four superimposed triads. (CBDM,
1955, 7 pp.) About 10 min. Some MM & Ped.

7.28 DEVČÍC, NATKO. Micro-Suite (1965).
Has advantage of single twelve-tone set used clearly
with repetitions of a few sonorities. Set used twice in
original form, twice in retrograde. Ostinato is quiet
movement with only a few tones and many rests in RH
melody. Forte stresses rapidly repeated clusterlike
chords. Some measures have 1/4 plus 6/16 meter
signatures. Arpeggiato achieves grace through flexible
rhythms with irregular groupings and harmonic seconds. Hands alternate rapidly in Quasi Una Cadenza.

(In 7. 2, 3 pp.)   4 movements.   MM, some Ped.

7. 29 DUBOIS, PIERRE MAX.   Hommage à Poulenc.
Pleasant, unassuming, and skillful. Graceful melodies
move usually by step.   Except for Maestoso introduction, first and last pages are Allegro "white key" music with melody centered in e phrygian mode.   LH
two-beat ostinato includes gentle sevenths and seconds.
Warmer harmonies of middle two pages are frequently
centered on g-sharp.   Ninth reach essential.   (Led,
1963, 4 pp.) 3 min, 30 sec.

7. 30 DUKE, VERNON.   Parisian Suite (1955).
Attractive pieces can be very useful: if youthful performer's interest strays from music, sophisticated,
chromatic harmonies should lure attention back.   Titles
such as An American Girl and Lovers, Lovers Every-
where are hard to resist.   Despite lightness and humor,
works are serious.   Full textures provide excellent keyboard practice.   A Spinster on a Bicycle has a "breath-
lessly" rapid RH near-perpetual motion with much variety of finger patterns, including some extensions.
Lively LH, with some tango rhythms, enhances light
mood.   Harmonies lead in and out of many keys.   Sunday Outing has appealing harmonies for attractive melodies.   Keys of B-flat, A-flat and B.   6/8 and 3/4
meters combined in one passage, as well as two melodies which first appeared separately.   Numerous octaves, also thirds.   Cafe Flore Intellectual is not too
serious a fugal style, hinting at spuriousness by the
direction "unhappily;" also, a curious harmonic shift
occurs as subject ends, and second, third, and fourth
entries are made at intervals of major sixth, diminished fifth, and minor sixth.   The Paris intellectual
must, indeed, be surfeited because counterpoint is
sometimes abandoned for "nice" sounding homophony.
The "quasi polka" An Old Boulevardier has quick-shift-
ing oom-pah bass.   Flippant melodies and sleek harmonic changes suggest artful spoof.   In D-flat, G-flat
and F.   (BrB, 1956, 23 pp.) 10 pieces.   12 min, 14
sec.   7, some 6 & 8.

7. 31 EKLUND, HANS.   Fantasia (1962).
Molto lento chordal proclamations have decided emotional impact.   Doubly inflected chords progress by
step; between chordal measures a lone line (sometimes
coupled) in severe dotted rhythm or rhapsodic rush

promotes sober mood. (In 5.5, 2 pp.) Some Ped.

7.32 ESCHER, RUDOLF. Sonatina, Op. 20 (1951).
Facile, finely integrated neo-classic work. Precise
pedal indications (both full and half) in French, English,
and German give clues to concern for exact textures
and idiomatic piano writing. Allegro assai is indeed
"always with grace." Texture is varied, with parallel common chords and coupled writing for contrast in
middle section. Serious, yet appealing Molto tranquillo is marked "bright and expressive, but always
rigorously in tempo." ABA in form, A imitative, the
short B homophonic. A begins with a one-line phrase,
which is transposed down a step three times, but ends
each time on the same A-flat chord with added second.
Much treble register. "Resolute and regulated" movement III is very rapid, extrovert, and effective. One
pleasant idea, or one type of passage work, fluently
succeeds another. Many harmonic and broken triads.
Rhythms of three against two. (Al, 1952, 20 pp.) 3
movements. MM, Ped. 7, some 6.

7.33 FINNEY, ROSS LEE. Nostalgic Waltzes.
Utterly charming work will develop interpretative
taste. Expressive aims are transparent but sophisti-
catedly varied. Moods suggested by such directions
as "chattery" and "conversational." Tonal harmonies,
with keys like c-sharp and e-flat, include suave chromaticisms and modulations; more contemporary harmonies like momentary polyharmonies. Effective, traditional pianism used, including hand and finger staccato, thirds and octaves, precise pedaling and singing
tone. John Kirkpatrick edits the work explicitly, including directions for rubato. The five Waltzes are
intended as a unit. Lovely baritone melody in middle
section of slow fourth Waltz, marked "simply and naturally," is one demonstration of Waltzes' nostalgic
quality. First and last sections use same eight-measure "parlando" strain five times, arranged differently
and sometimes transposed. Acc has repeated bell-
like tone. Coda's tonic chord has gentle bite from
doubly inflected third and added seventh. Concluding
Waltz, admirably unified, has two moods: one is
"boisterous" with melody in octaves leaping about
among chord tones accompanied by full-texture traditional waltz bass; alluring second mood is "slippery"
or "slick" with a prominent three-note figure. Pian-

istic embellishments throughout add to rousing finish.
(Merc, 1953, 16 pp.) Fngr, MM, some Ped. 7 & 8.

7.34 FROIDEBISE, PIERRE. Hommage à Chopin (1947).
Charming, effective, and very musical twelve-tone
waltz. Set includes five fourths; natural consequence
is tonal cadence in B several times. Twelve-tone writing quite strict, although in middle poetic section an inner pedal wavers between two tones a major second
apart; in the same section LH frequently crosses over
RH. Treble melody has splendid lyrical line with much
interval variety. Acc has either a few widely-spaced
intervals or shorter staccato or legato tones with extensions. Precise and varied dynamics. Wide keyboard range. Rhythmically traditional. (CBDM, 1955,
5 pp.) 4 min. MM, Ped.

7.35 GAZOULEAS, STEPHANOS. Klavierstück (1965).
Absorbing Piano Piece is study in rhythm and sonority.
Fascinating sounds of densely-textured atonal harmonies
can be relished because of repetition. Three staves
used. Notated in 4/4, music playfully toys with concept of ordinary beats: one-quarter of the beats do
have a beginning sound impact, but one-third of the
beats are anticipated or delayed by one-quarter or one-
third of the beat. Result is a wonderfully fluid motion.
Melody of little importance. (In 7.1, 2 pp.) MM,
Ped.

7.36 GOLEMINOV, MARIN. Bulgarian Dance.
Approachable Allegro con brio number has splendid variety. Fluid rhythms, with meter changes amid constant motion. Much dynamic interest. Frequent forearm staccatos. In f. Motto translation is: "Watch
out, Earth, a wealthy farmer passes by." (In 6.2, 3
pp.) MM, some Ped. Biog.

7.37 GRAMATGES, HAROLD. Dos Danzas Cubanas.
Two Cuban Dances combine typical Latin American allure with skillful craftsmanship. Both Allegro moderato
pieces have many legato double notes, particularly thirds
and sixths; RH outside fingers play the melody. Much
syncopation, particularly with tones tied across beats.
Form of Country Dance (1) is ABACA, with introduction
and coda; longer C is made up of four slightly varied
sections, one utilizing a fragment of A. Successions
of eight eighth notes within the 2/4 measures are

grouped frequently by three and five because of accents. Some staccato provides contrast to usual legato. Sonera (Dance Singer?) (2) is charming with
warm colors of D-flat. Six sections of different material appear in varying order; at the end first three
sections reappear in reverse order. Each hand may
be rhythmically displaced a sixteenth note early or
late, providing elusive harmony. Phrases seldom end
on a beat. (Peer, 1953, 10 pp.) MM. 7 & 8.

7.38 GUARNIERI, M. CAMARGO. Improviso (1948).
"Calmo" intention is admirably realized in this Improvisation. Noticeable throughout is syncopated South
American rhythm, with tones on last half of second
beat tied through beginning of third beat. LH has
small-range melody in A section of the ABA form; in
bell-like acc a melody tone serves also for a slow-
moving bass while RH has repeated octave acc above
the melody. In B, similar to A, melody is in outer
RH fingers, but B is more intense with fuller texture
and counter melody. Conservative tonal harmony.
(Ric-Br, 1957, 4 pp.) MM.

7.39 GUARNIERI, M. CAMARGO. Valsa No. 7 (1954).
Marked "languishing," this beautiful Waltz unfolds a
moderately chromatic melodic line. Main melody is
in bass of A sections of strict ABA form. Harmony
has some fourth chords, and a counter melody gradually develops in RH. Faster B has ornamented, steady
eighth note treble melody; counter melody emerges at
the end, predicted earlier because of moderately jagged line. Concern for bass line apparent. Hand staccato in RH. (Ric-Br, 1957, 5 pp.) Fngr, MM.

7.40 HATRÍK, JURAJ. Malá Suita.
Small Suite is charming, with unexpected turns. Musically transparent work is unassumingly original. Homophonic texture although very few chords used. Tonal
and conservative. Three pairs of pieces are grouped
by attacca direction. 2 is a lovely Lento rubato; lyrical treble melody is recitative in nature, the whimsical acc using a patterned three-note figure. Tranquillo allegro non troppo 3 has resourceful textures:
at first RH alternates between treble melody and accompanying chromatic bass flourish, while LH has
rapid pp notated trill and chromatic counter melody.
After "resolute," dissonant slower section, opening

material reappears in same slow tempo as a coda.   7,
marked "Lento rubato e espressive," has recitativelike
melody coupled two octaves apart; its short stretches
begin with upward flashing arpeggios of exotic nonhar-
monic coloring.   Directions are that arpeggios, divided
between the hands, begin before the beat.   Delightful
Vivacissimo e con bravura 8 is scherzo in nature.
RH technique requires rapid repeated single notes or
thirds and trill-like thirds.   Concluding superimposed
fifths, preceded by fifths half step away, suggest similar non-harmonic radiance heard throughout.   (Pan,
1966, 21 pp.)   8 movements.   Ped.   7, some 5 & 6.

7.41   HELPS, ROBERT.   Recollections.
Nothing routine about these exquisitely crafted works.
Composer has perceptive ear for piano sonorities with
wide pitch range and much texture variety.   Serious
In Memoriam is usually anchored by repeated rhythms
of slowly changing harmonies.   Fragmented melody,
with many rests, has numerous unrelated descending
fourths.   Interlude (seven pages) is related to impressionism.   Beginning and end have rapid tremolos in
both hands which create a sheen of usually pp coloring.
Middle section more intense.   Lento rubato Epilogue
has expressive improvisatory measures, partly unified
by descending or ascending melodic second, alone or
ending a longer fragment.   A motive repeated in two
registers emerges briefly.   Tonality suggested at end
by low repeated B's.   Non-tonal; harmonies include triads and seventh chords.   Extreme range and constantly
changing piano style.   (Pet 66167, 1968, 15 pp.)   3
pieces.   15 min.   MM, Ped.   7, some 6.

7.42   HODDINOTT, ALUN.   Second Nocturne, Op. 16, No. 1.
Molto Adagio of astonishing variety.   Rhapsodic mood
includes both the mystic or impressionistic and spurts
of ff display.   Ornate treble line, sometimes coupled,
often has no acc.   Precise rhythm notation, with eighth
note constant; among variety of beat subdivisions are
thirty-second notes and triplets of sixteenths.   Many
harmonic thirds.   Clear emphasis of E-flat indicates
piece in that key.   (Nov, 1964, 4 pp.)   Ped.

7.43   HOVHANESS, ALAN.   Fantasy on an Ossetin Tune,
        Op. 85, No. 6 (1951).
Hypnotizes with exotic appeal.   Ossets are a people of
the central Caucasus.   First two pages serve as pre-

lude before main theme "in dance style;" introduction
is both measured and unmeasured, with music started
and broken off by faster roulades until it accelerates
to last four pages of Allegro perpetual motion. Theme
then heard six times; first three times the essentially
coupled line is accompanied by broken chord acciaccaturas which gradually disappear during fourth time, re-
placed by melody alternating rapidly with a repeated
drone, probably simulating plucking of native instrument. Rapid hand alternation continues in a non-the-
matic section, dynamics gradually building to last two
returns of theme. Coupled hands have rotary motion
to ff ending. Beats divided by two through six in challenging mixes. Mode of last four pages resembles
phrygian on e, with frequent raised second and sixth
and lowered fifth. (Peer, 1957, 6 pp.) Ped.

7.44 HOVHANESS, ALAN. Mazert Nman Rehani, Op. 38.
Thy Hair Is Like Basil Leaf depicts "Taxim (a wandering, improvisational spirit) for piano imitating the
kanoon (similar to a zither), the tar (a plucked instrument), and the oud (lute). " Rhapsodic mood of one-
line music is captured by fast unmeasured and measured sections. Many repeated tones, notated trills,
and broken octaves. Rapid even exchanges between
hands, with RH much busier throughout. Indications
for pedal release only at numerous rests. Centered
on A with prominent augmented second between b-flat
and c-sharp. Perpetual motion of last two pages builds
to fff climax. (Pet 6640a, 1968, 10 pp.) Some MM
& Ped.

7.45 HOVHANESS, ALAN. Mountain Dance No. 2, Op. 144b.
Exotic, easy-to-understand somber work has splendid
consistency and useful technical requirements. All
tones restricted to a mode on g like the dorian, except that an augmented second is gained by raising
fourth step. Practice for cluster chords, very rapid
RH scale passages, and moderately fast coupled octaves. Dynamic variety from ppp to f. (Pet 6278,
1964, 3 pp.) 3 min. MM, Ped.

7.46 HUSA, KARL. Élégie.
Elegy is impassioned work with strange intangible qualities. "Quasi improvisando. " Essentially in C, freely
using all twelve tones. Beginning and ending one line
only, the ending a retrograde of first; intense middle,

emphasizing dominant tone G, climaxes with varied
fast reiterations of octaves or one chord.   Supple
rhythms.   (Led, 1968, 2 pp.)   4 min, 30 sec.   MM,
Ped.

7.47 IŠTVAN, MILOŠ.   Odyssey of a Child of Lidice.
Moving and wonderfully integrated moderate tempo
piece.   Bell sonorities implied throughout.   Motives
are introduced unassumingly; some repetitions are obvious, but most are skillfully changed.   Work begins
with enchanting upper register sonorities blended by
fairly long pedals, succeeded by clashing fifths and
seconds which become acc later for declamatory fragments.   Thinner texture passage unified by upper harmonic minor second is followed by linear counterpoint
in octaves, then a transformed recapitulation.   Foreword in Czech, German, and English states "the in-
spiration for the composition was the fate of the children of Lidice who were torn from their homes and after long years of wandering were returned to their
families."   "The tone organization is partly serial,
partly modal."   Footnote translation on page nine is
"the sixteenth note is somewhat compressed, and the
last tone must be lengthened, so that the accompanying line remains rhythmically firm."   (SHV, 1966, 7
pp.)   5 min.   MM, Ped.

7.48 JELINEK, HANNS.   Six Short Character-Sketches, Op.
      15, No. 2 (1947).
Twelve-tone music manages also to be entertaining.
Same set used untransposed throughout in original order.   Edition gives the set and titles and directions in
German, English, and French.   "... by means of the
same form of line the most contrasting characters are
represented."   Fluently (also in 4.9 and 8.3) is in two
lines, RH leading.   One voice almost always holds a
tone while the second moves.   Fluttering is humorous-
ly depicted by rapid wide-spaced flourishes up and down
the keyboard and by skips in the melody.   Beautiful
Singing (also in 4.9) is just that.   Lyrical treble melody and often repeated two and three-tone chordal acc.
(UE 11899, 1951, 7 pp.)   3 min, 25 sec.   MM.   7,
some 5 & 6.

7.49 JELINEK, HANNS.   Sonatine, Op. 9, Nr. 4.
Intensely expressive work in predominantly chromatic
Viennese idiom.   Tempos and dynamics constantly

change to capture many lyrical or intense moods.
Much secondary contrapuntal interest in support of
principal lyrical line. Moderato assai first movement
has clear form. First five-note motive significant.
Tonal awareness in second motive using broken triad,
in the fifth relationship in repeats, and at final cadence. Fourth chords. After Menuett and Introduction, Vivo Rondino is playful conclusion to more involved preceding movements. Almost classic features
include broken thirds, metrical patterns, and coupled
writing. Enchanting treble sonorities in contrasting
Tranquillo section. (UE 11916, 1951, 9 pp.) 4 movements. 8 min, 30 sec. MM. 7, some 6 & 8.

7.50 JELINEK, HANNS. Three Dances, Op. 15, No. 3
      (1947).
      Expressive, varied works are moderately contempo-
      rary. Each piece uses one untransposed transforma-
      tion of single twelve-tone set, with much repetition of
      two or more tones before proceeding to next tone.
      Composer provides many directions. Edition gives
      the set and identifies the transformations with direc-
      tions in German, English, and French. Waltz is
      charming piece of spontaneous Viennese moods. Flex-
      ible changes include much rubato. Lyric Sarabande
      concerned with two melodies and their repetitions,
      either by ornamented variation or by inversion. Poly-
      phonic interest. Direction to make "melody very
      prominent." March is grotesque and usually severe.
      Often in a low register. Wide reach helpful. (UE
      11900, 1951, 12 pp.) 9 min, 15 sec. MM. 7, some
      6.

7.51 KLEBE, GISELHER. Drei Romanzen, Op. 43 (1963).
      Three Romances are twelve-tone works of integrity.
      Interesting to performer who searches. Writing var-
      ied and very detailed. Rests important. Generally
      gentle rather than intense. I is a Larghetto with Piu
      mosso middle section. Some arresting chords. First
      section is most often dolce. The appassionato middle
      has polyrhythms, such as groups of three or four with
      a group of five. Insistent broken major sevenths or
      minor ninths in acc. II is an Allegretto assai, and
      Largo. Compelling line in first section. Texture has
      either two voices or striking, gradually accumulating
      cluster chords. III, marked "with elegiac sentiment,"
      is more accessible than I or II. Ground bass often

present. Simple rhythms. (B&B, 1964, 8 pp.) 8
min. MM, some Ped. 7, some 6.

7.52 KLEBE, GISELHER. Wiegenlieder für Christinchen,
      Op. 13 (1952).
Lullabies for Christine are fanciful, sensitive, and
erudite. For the most dedicated. Twelve-tone influenced. German preface indicates pieces are written
according to variable meter system (I basically moves
from a measure in three through five, seven, eleven
and thirteen, or the reverse); pauses between pieces
are to be brief, and metronome marks are to be
strictly observed. Small note values must be counted,
with endings sometimes on very short notes. Prevailing dynamics are soft, with none above mf. Fragments of mirror and retrograde writing. III seems
ever changing; however, there is frequent use of accompanying first inversion triad with two inflections
of the third and without fifth, as well as reappearances
of notated trills, tremolos and chromatic scales. V
continuously unfolds new ideas, with repeated single
tones filling out to cluster chords and two-part passage
work coalescing in coupled writing. More accessible
VI has many different note values. Included are quick
streaks over the keyboard, initially one-line using all
twelve tones, then two voices in contrary motion with
upper voice using the last six tones in retrograde.
IX has three sections using different material. Each
section partly unified by repeated rhythms. First section has quick-note passages in which four set transformations occur, one measure intervening. Last section quotes from the quick streaks of VI. "Basic unit"
is first the sixteenth, then thirty-second, and then six-
teenth--relationships remaining constant. German directions in II indicate that fermata lengths should vary
and in VIII that fermatas should be long and as uniform
as possible. (B&B, 1953, 14 pp.) 9 pieces. 12 min.
MM, some Ped. 7 & 8.

7.53 KOHS, ELLIS B. Variations on "L'Homme Armé"
      (1946-1947).
Effective, brilliant and straightforward music of long
tradition. Theme is the first nine measures of the
noble French folk song often used as a cantus firmus
in the fifteenth and sixteenth centuries. Treatment in
the eighteen variations is in the manner of English vir-
ginal patterned variations, each variation using a dis-

tinct keyboard technique.   Frequent rapid double notes
with one note repeated and RH rapid scale passages.
Stretch of a ninth a necessity.   Many fifths, fourths,
open octaves and harsh, bare dissonances like medieval
modal harmonies.   End states the theme again very
softly.   Page turning may be troublesome.   (Merc,
1962, 8 pp.)   Some Ped.

7.54   KÖLZ, ERNST.   Sonate (1951).
Obsessed with stark, primitive energy and simplicity.
Repetitive drumbeats.   Outer movements very fast,
middle very slow.   Harmony of first sonata form movement has two superimposed fifths in parallel motion,
or fifths with added seconds, sixths, etc.   Melody always moves by step.   6/8 and 8/8 usually, with irregular rests.   Slow movement is like some primeval
chant.   Parallel chords of two fifths change to awkward
bass melody, followed by incessant bass octave or seventh accompanying strokes.   Hypnotic fourth and fifth
repetitions in last movement varied by alternating
strokes between hands and irregular accents.   Frequent
meter changes.   Irresistible forward push.   (UE 12065,
1951, 8 pp.)   3 movements.   MM.   7, some 6.

7.55   KOPTAGEL, YÜKSEL.   Tamzara.
Musically forthright, moderately fast Turkish dance.
Splendid for octaves.   4/8 and 5/8 meters (two and
three or the reverse) combined in 9/8 measure.   Aeolian mode on d and e-flat, with acc often raising sixth
and seventh steps.   Two stepwise melodic ideas used in
well-knit construction: four-measure phrases shortened
to two and then one-measure repetitions for increasing
excitement.   Numerous accidental signs omitted: correct notes should be obvious.   (Esc, 1960, 4 pp.)   MM.

7.56   KOPTAGEL, YÜKSEL.   Toccata.
Maximum effect attained for means used; obvious, sounding more difficult than it is.   Fascinating play of
rhythms: indication is that 5/8 and 4/8 are combined
to make 9/8, but this frequently breaks down.   6/8 and
3/8 are regularly combined.   Only sixteen times in the
175 measures of the work do two successive measures
continue the same meter.   In a, with frequent bass motion by fifth or second.   Some cross relation.   Much
hand alternation.   Some parallel sixths.   Numerous octaves, usually not in immediate succession.   (Esc,
1960, 7 pp.)

7.57 McCABE, JOHN. <u>Five Bagatelles</u> (1964).
Twelve-tone works of distinct and varied character have
jagged lines and short phrases.   Foreword about serial music in general.   Each work clearly repeats material and reveals other procedures of construction.
Set often introduced gradually in melodies, repeated
fragments binding separated material together.   Melody
and chordal acc usually distinct from each other.   Eloquent <u>Elegia</u> has improvisatory melody with much variety of half-note beat divisions.   Three acc four-tone
chords only, totalling one complete set.   Slashing Con
brio and ritmico <u>Toccata</u> has alternations between chord
proclamations and rapid, widely-spaced descending and
ascending one-line runs.   Four-tone chordal passages
tend to have seconds, thirds, or sixths in each hand.
Chords of last half are repeated from first half, while
runs mirror those occurring earlier.   (Elk, 1964, 6
pp.) MM, some Ped. Anal. 7, some 5 & 6.

7.58 MALIPIERO, G. FRANCESCO. <u>Variazione</u> (1959).
Lento <u>Variations</u> on the Pantomime from <u>Falla's El</u>
<u>Amor Brujo</u> use the first three back-and-forth pitches
of the slow flute melody.   The two-measure fragment
is almost always present, often in acc.   Form is fluid,
so that the end of a variation usually is not explicit.
Harmony is very opaque, with evidence of tonality only
in the final long bass plagal cadence, complicated by
unrelated theme tripled in treble and doubled in contrary motion below.   Texture varies from two voices
to three-tone chords in each hand.   Middle ranges only. (Ch, 1960, 3 pp.)

7.59 MARTINON, JEAN. <u>Sonatine No. 3,</u> Op. 22 (1940).
Charming work is melodically and harmonically ingratiating in the French manner.   Many fertile ideas.
Added note, seventh through thirteenth, and altered
chords.   Much rhythmic variety, although no more nov-
el than changing meters or a 15/8 meter grouped as
five, five, five or three, three, three, three, three
indicated by figures 5 or 3 above the staff.   Pianistically very smooth, with skillful blend of full and thin
sounds.   First fast movement is in sonata allegro
form, with development resembling a free fantasia; recapitulation of second idea occurs before the first.   Expressivo, leggiero, and dolce directions suggest
warmth of the movement.   In the short Adagio, textures vary from two voices to seven-note chords.   ABA

form <u>Scherzo</u> has graceful and flexible coupled writing
skillfully varied by other textures. In middle Meno
vivo section parallel harmonies over rocking 7/8 acc
provide enchanting sonorities. (Bil, 1951, 12 pp.) 3
movements. 8 min. Some MM & Ped. 7, some 6.

7.60 MARTINŮ, BOHUSLAV. <u>Les Bouquinistes du Quai</u>
     <u>Malaquais</u> (1948).
<u>Booksellers</u> of Quay Malaquais is accessible Allegro.
Variety of piano textures include coupled writing one
and three octaves apart and rapid notes in both hands
in contrary motion. Slurring contrary to the beat and
rotary motion also used. In F. Conservative. (Heu,
1954, 3 pp.)

7.61 MARTINŮ, BOHUSLAV. <u>The Fifth Day of the Fifth</u>
     <u>Moon.</u>
Marvellous evocation of sounds typical of Chinese music. Often in pentatonic mode, many bell sounds.
Ancient Chinese poem included in English and French.
Music progresses from impassive melody accompanied
by extended broken fifths through fuller texture, including harmonic fourths and fifths, to ff climax of polychords. More ornate f section has near-coupled writing in interesting disagreement and a long trill with
broken fifth acc. End repeats the beginning. (Heu,
1951, 4 pp.)

7.62 MATHIAS, WILLIAM. <u>Toccata alla Danza</u> (1961).
Effective Allegro vivo varies between vigorous jabs and
enchanting bell-like upper peals with long held pedal.
Rhythms are agile with changing meters and patterns
against the meter; rhythms sometimes altered even
when pitch pattern repeated. Frequent return to d
tonal center, spiced by c-sharps; percussive added-
note, quartal, and polychordal harmonies. Linear
principle; motion often stepwise toward some tempo-
rary goal, with little thought for harmonies along the
way. Some mirror writing. Varied articulations.
Some quick RH ostinato passages with many fourths.
Each hand is equally busy with single, double, or
triple notes; moderately full texture. Commissioned
by Welsh Committee of Arts Council. (Oxf, 1965, 6
pp.) 3 min. Ped.

7.63 MONTSALVATGE, XAVIER. <u>Three Divertissements.</u>
Slyly entertaining numbers of obvious tune and har-

mony built "on Themes of Forgotten Composers."
Popular elements are dressed up with clever polytonalities, enharmonic modulations, and wayward chromaticisms. Tongue-in-cheek music has traditional piano
styles and rhythms. Title also in Spanish. I is diatonic, like a Sousa march with two "boring" develop-
ments over ostinatos. LH back-and-forth acc. II is
a languid habanera in A-flat. Chords have some double
inflections. RH double notes include weak-finger melody. III is an hilarious Vivo. Sensitive coloring will
bring out the musical humor. Flourishes of repeated
rhythms, chromatic scales, and minor seconds romp-
ing up and down the keyboard. Middle section is cantabile. (SMP, 1955, 8 pp.) 7, some 6.

7.64 MOORE, DOUGLAS. Barn Dance.
Allegro robusto of splendid spirit, integrity, and consistency. Eight-measure tune with prominent fourths
is heard thirteen times (and with remarkable interest)
in increasingly complex settings. Always in F, varying with mixtures of aeolian, dorian, mixolydian or
major modes; otherwise very few accidentals. Pianistic features include forearm and hand staccatos, octaves, LH back-and-forth motion, and moderately full
chords. (CF, 1951, 4 pp.) Some Fngr, MM.

7.65 MOORE, DOUGLAS. Dancing School.
Straightforward, strongly melodic work. Melody is
tripled or quadrupled, with some climactic register
shifts. Acc in each hand usually double notes on off-
beats. Alternates between triple and duple meters.
Hand and forearm staccato. In E-flat and D (very few
accidentals) with middle section "in the manner of a
Viennese Waltz." (CF, 1951, 6 pp.) Fngr, MM, Ped.

7.66 MOORE, DOUGLAS. Procession.
Splendid staccato and legato chord study. "With steady
menacing beat throughout" describes its grim forward
tread. Tonic tone f often reiterated in the bass. Staccato widely-spaced chords and successive or simultaneous cross relations reinforce the forbidding mood. A
glimmer of hope looms gradually in middle section but
somber mood prevails at the end in insistent ff. (CF,
1951, 6 pp.) Fngr, MM, Ped.

7.67 MUCZYNSKI, ROBERT. Six Preludes, Op. 6.
Attractive light-hearted grotesqueries and drive are

like Prokofieff.   Percussive staccato harmonies and
dissonances.   Effective and pianistic.   Wide range
used.   Tonal, with all twelve tones freely used.   Neo-
classic.   Five are fast.   II is a solemn, mysterious
Lento of impressive compositional skill.   RH near-
ostinato of broken ninths and octaves gently collides
against LH varied harmonies in middle range and low
tonic and dominant pedal tones.   Energetic, Allegro
giocoso III will develop RH hand staccato and strength
on scalar or broken chord melody.   LH jabs against
RH half step away with octaves or single tones.   Either in all bass or all treble register.   Ostinato patterns.   Allegro moderato VI is neo-primitive music of
much animation.   Always staccato.   Many octaves.
Constant eighth note motion has irregular accents.
Range usually low.   (II and VI are also in 8. 4.)   (GS,
1961, 15 pp.)   MM, Ped. 7, some 5 & 6.

7.68 ORGAD, BEN ZION.   Two Preludes in Impressionistic
        Mood (1960).
      Evocative of some ancient plaint.   Economical.   Very
      broadly tonal.   Title and biography in Hebrew and Eng-
      lish.   Lento I begins and ends in mood of deliberation
      created by repeated sonorities like fourths and sev-
      enths.   Middle more active with semi-parallel third-
      less chords and repeated note acc.   Moderato rubato
      II starts forlornly with treble melody doubled two oc-
      taves away accompanied by short rhythmic snippets.
      Middle section, marked Animato, has f melodic jabs
      and dissonant near-cluster chords.   (IMI, 1967, 7 pp.)
      7 min.   *Biog.

7.69 PALAU, MANUEL.   Evocación de Andalucía.
      Bright, volatile Presto.   Attractive, typically Spanish
      music calls for graceful interpretation.   Fine variety
      between staccato, thinly accompanied textures and
      pedaled legato, moderately full textures.   Much treble
      range.   Usually diatonic, in f-sharp.   Conservative.
      Direction translations are "freely" and "simply sing-
      ing" (p 1), "with emphasis" (p 3), "expressive" (p 4),
      and "ritard a little," (p 5).   (UME, 1954, 7 pp.)
      MM, some Ped.

7.70 PALMER, ROBERT.   Three Epigrams (1957-1958).
      Polished neo-classic, but original music, aptly titled.
      Tonal, with all twelve tones freely used.   Static, near
      ostinato measures remind one of Stravinsky.   Many

details, particularly in I and III. Meter changes frequently, especially in I and II. Usually f or less in
dynamics. Ninth reach. Use of sostenuto pedal indi-
cated--editing by John Kirkpatrick. I is an Allegretto
grazioso often with RH chords grouped by two and three
and LH ostinato usually by three. Tones of RH chords
often move only in inner voice. LH has forearm staccato extensions. Harmonic complexities like polyharmonies eventually are centered in C. II is a puckish
Agitato ma leggiero with splendid plan of motion, building to a sustained chord. Patterned rhythms, often
dotted. III is a lyrical Andante con moto of subtle un-
derstatement. Blues notes reveal appealing allusions
to jazz. Polyrhythms of two against three. (Peer,
1960, 12 pp.) Ped. 7, some 6.

7.71 PAPP, LAJOS. Three Rondos.
Combine direct, primitive appeal with easily assimilated sophistication. Faster first and third numbers
have robust vitality. Coupled and two-part coupled
writing included in effective texture variety--whole is
fluently pianistic. Flexibly tonal--individual harmonies
often traditional, but freely chromatic contrapuntal motion usually prevents clear tonal identification. Main
meter is 6/8. Title also in Hungarian and German.
Total form of fluent Allegro I is ABCA with coda. A
contains melodic fourths, small extensions, treble first
inversion triads with dissonant bass, and coupled fifths
moving up and down by minor thirds. B has RH passages containing notated trills and a bass ostinato of
broken staccato ninths. C is in 5/8 with ascending
scale patterns slurred each two beats. Varied articulations include forearm staccatos. In Andante 2,
marked legatissimo, cross relations suggest polyharmony. Lyrical, small-range treble melody unfolds
logically. Double note acc. (EMB, 1967, 10 pp.)
Some MM & Ped. 7, some 6.

7.72 PARTOS, OEDOEN. Prelude (1960).
Bold-gestured work of rhapsodic variety. Octaves and
coupled writing very effective. Rubato and much varied
note values. Bar lines used but no meter signatures.
Moves in short spurts, rests interrupting. Exotic fragments like melismatic chants. Repeated dense intervals fill out to cluster chords. Twelve-tone set
emerges haphazardly at end. Biography in Hebrew and
English. (IMI, 1968, 4 pp.) 5 min. MM. *Biog.

7.73 PASCAL, ANDRÉ. Cloches des Vosges.
Bells of the Vosges (Mountains) will appeal to those
who respond to piquant harmonies in full chordal texture.   Melody introduced in parallel harmonization
used by the carillon of a clock factory "in a sonority
of far away bells."   Parallel fourths continue in the
main section "like a popular song;" acc is lovely brok-
en chords in either hand.   Gentle, popular harmonic
coloring from parallel added-note, fourth, polychords,
and doubly inflected chords.   Practice in reading many
accidentals.   (Esc, 1951, 2 pp.)

7.74 PERLE, GEORGE. Six Preludes, Op. 20B (1946).
Expressiveness will be demanding; understanding requires persistence.   Except for IV, bar lines are few
and far between; prose rhythms varied but not particularly difficult.   Tonalities very elusive; common but
unrelated chords appear frequently.   First three Preludes have much dynamic contrast; dynamics more uniform in the last three.   II has sporadic, rapid descending LH arpeggios.   Slashing harmonic seconds and
sevenths, sometimes repeated, are important in IV.
"Sempre forte e senza espressivo" broken chords of V
are strictly organized--last half is first half in mirror
invertible counterpoint.   Disjunct melody in slow VI is
nearly twelve-tone; LH acc always harmonic sixths or
thirds.   (In 6.4, 4 pp.) MM, Ped. 7, some 6 & 8.

7.75 POULENC, FRANCIS. XIVième Improvisation (1958).
Fourteenth Improvisation, in D-flat, is lovely lyrical
Allegretto.   Undemonstrative and secure, seeming to
say "Here I am," with no further ado.   RH weak fingers play the melody as part of moderately full chords,
never exceeding f.   Smooth harmonies modulate often--
from D-flat to E, G, B, E-flat, g, G-flat and back to
D-flat for entire last third.   Enharmonic modulations;
sometimes chromatic.   Several directions indicate music is to be played "strictly in the same tempo from
beginning to end." (Sal, 1958, 3 pp.) MM.

7.76 POULENC, FRANCIS. Novelette in E Minor (1959).
Published as one of Three Nocturnes, this lovely work
on a theme from the Pantomime section of Falla's El
Amor Brujo has felicitous piano texture.   Melody in
treble is accompanied by low bass tones and broken
chords; also by offbeat RH single tones or momentary
broken chords, all "bathed by pedals."   Fine study for

melody tone quality and subdued acc.   Harmonies become more adventuresome, with final three chords a
dominant seventh lowered a half step, usual dominant
seventh with added sixth, and tonic with added second,
raised sixth and lowered seventh.   Beautiful coda in
harmonic chords, "always without slowing." (Earlier
separately published Nocturnes in collection are in C
and b.) (Ches, 1960, 4 pp.) MM.

7.77 PROSTAKOFF, JOSEPH. Two Bagatelles.
Solid content and winsome appeal, undeniably contemporary. Atonal. I, marked Adagio molto e espressivo,
is partially a study in contrast between fleet, irregular one-line fragments in high register and lower, slow,
solemn chords. II is a Con moto with jazz influences,
suggested in repeated, syncopated bass tones. Essentially in two lines. Acc has extended broken-chord
grace notes, quickly released. (In 6.4, 3 pp.) MM.

7.78 QUINET, MARCEL. Hommage à Scarlatti (1962).
Pianistically facile pleasantries with sparkling high register, staccato writing. Often in two voices, one acc.
Frequent octave displacements, resulting in minor
ninths or major sevenths. Dynamics usually less than
f. Allegrammente, ABA in form, has some cluster
chord acc. Fine practice for staccato leaps, rotary
motion, and rapid passage work involving both extensions and scales. Cantabile has many legato extensions and harmonic seconds in the acc. Well-labelled
Giocoso is merry with two and three-note figures using
extensions. (CBDM, 1963, 20 pp.) 3 movements.   7
min. Some MM. 7, some 6.

7.79 RAMOVŠ, PRIMOŽ. Prelude.
Striking ebb and flow of harmonic tension in slow tempo. Thin texture of twelve different melody tones with
little or no acc changes to harmonic denseness of eight-
tone cluster chords. Dense areas also have many harmonic seconds, fourths, and sevenths. Often long
damper pedals and loud dynamics. Wide pitch range
and noticeable dissonances. (In 7.2, 3 pp.) MM,
Ped.

7.80 RIEGGER, WALLINGFORD. Toccata.
Allegro tour de force of constantly alternating hands.
In the perpetual sixteenth note motion LH is on the
beat. Originally entitled Fourths and Fifths, LH fifths

are usually on black keys with two superimposed
fourths of RH usually on white keys close by.   Positions sometimes awkward.   Dynamics are mostly f or
louder.   Moderate endurance developed.   Ending revised from original version, taken from composer's
New and Old collection.   (B&H, 1957, 4 pp.)

7. 81 SAKAC, BRANIMIR.   Variation.
Surprisingly accessible Allegretto moderato, after acquaintance.   Title may stem from varied use of rhythmic motive of two sixteenths and an eighth or from
melodic and harmonic fourth repetitions.   Linear counterpoint.   Distantly tonal, with much chromaticism.
(In 7. 2, 2 pp.)   Some Ped.

7. 82 SAVAGNONE, GIUSEPPE.   Preludio N. 1 (1955).
Flamboyant Prelude No. 1 from Harmonic Prism is
like a bold cadenza.   Accessible, sounding more difficult than it is.   Often a single rhapsodic line requiring
strong fingers.   Motto of three descending tones.   Free
combination of loose twelve-tone and tonal writing.   Unusual to have complete twelve-tone set; its order usually changes.   Tonal suggestions come partially from
thirds and fourths in lines, mostly from strong bass
octaves; same c-sharp chord repeated at end.   Translation on p 3 is "excited."   (Ric, 1959, 3 pp.) MM,
Ped.

7. 83 SCHISKE, KARL.   Sonatine, Op. 42 (1954).
Vigorous, dramatic work shows splendid craftsmanship.
Progresses by manipulations such as inversions, re-
versal of roles of hands, ostinato, and union of previ-
ously separate material.   Transition material as striking as main material.   Thin textures, mostly staccato
tones.   Tempos usually fast.   Numerous meter changes.
Tonal, with free use of all twelve tones.   Melodic
fourths important.   Splendid for hand staccatos, independence, and equality.   In opening Allegro the first
theme vaults upward and downward by fourths.   Second
idea uses pp major sevenths.   Section conclusions clear
with cluster-chord repetitions.   Impressively logical
second movement begins Andante with slow-moving line
imitated by inversion; music moves to much faster tempo unified by bass ostinato of six measures, each in a
different meter.   Without changing pace first idea accompanied by diatonic pedal and D-flat scales; final
measures continue theme in frenzy of ff dissonant chord-

al jabs. All ideas of closing Allegretto again striking.
The pp ending is in keeping with movement's light
play. (Dob, 1956, 11 pp.) 3 movements. MM. 7 &
8, some 6.

7.84 SGRIZZI, LUCIANO. Ostinati (1956).
Pleasantly sophisticated; typically Italian direct appeal.
Repeated LH formulas. In Italian foreword composer
explains that Ostinato means also that succeeding numbers must follow with almost no break. He suggests
ten different orders of at least four numbers if whole
set isn't played. Tonal; frequent parallel harmonies.
Skillful piano writing. II, in the tempo of a waltz, has
an ostinato of minor triads. Some polyharmonies.
Many RH thirds; RH frequently crosses over LH. "A
little pedal every measure." V is an Allegro dolce e
poco rubato whose simple melody has exotic touches of
chromaticism, including tritones; may be doubled by
fourths or thirds. Ostinato emphasizes tritone. Excellent practice for strengthening outer fingers and
softening thumb. Pedal "every two quarters." Presto
"flowing" VI provides a compelling conclusion. In two
sections: ostinato in first has broken fourth pattern in
two against three; different ostinato in second section
with first ostinato gradually reappearing in RH. Hemiola rhythms also included in second section; RH at
times has four equal tones in the triple measure. In
c with variety between raised and lowered sixth degree; very few accidentals. Familiar ninth chords surface momentarily. (Zer, 1958, 18 pp.) 6 pieces. 8
min. MM, Ped. 7 & 8, some 6.

7.85 SICILIANOS, YORGO. Miniature, Op. 23, No. 7
(1963).
Charming and entertaining piece in waltz tempo, "burlesque but leggero." Facile melody has numerous
amusing leaps. Tonal; traditional acc usually thirds.
Treble range only, with melody and acc shifting between hands. Perhaps best for children, or young-at-
heart. Except for a few rapid leaps, piece level five
in difficulty. (In 7.1, 2 pp.) MM. Biog.

7.86 SKALKOTTAS, NIKOS. Suite for Piano No. 3.
Complex music because of harmony and full texture.
Harmonies are dissonant, dense, and uncompromising.
Familiar chords do emerge from very chromatic sur-
roundings. Forms are noticeably traditional. Wide

stretch helpful. <u>Minuetto</u> becomes increasingly under-
standable. Quartal harmonies at first, more tertian
at beginning of Trio. Rhythm is easily apparent.
Some lighter touches. Uses wide range of keyboard.
<u>Tema Con Variazoni</u> uses a "Greek popular theme"
with four variations and coda. Theme appears to be
in a-flat harmonic minor. Fragments of theme or
theme in inner parts can be discovered in variations.
<u>Marcia Funebre</u> and <u>Finale</u> complete the suite. (UE
13611, 1962, 8 pp.) 4 movements. Some MM.

7.87 SPIES, CLAUDIO. <u>Impromptu</u> (1963).
Wonderfully fragile, tender "cradle music." Marked
legato and dolce. Twelve-tone. Leaps, rests, and
rhythmic exactness indicate pointillistic writing. Not
really difficult when reading difficulties, such as rhythmic changes from 6/8 to 5/16, have been mastered.
(EV, 1964, 2 pp.) MM, Ped.

7.88 STARER, ROBERT. <u>Prelude</u> and <u>Toccata</u> (1946).
An undercurrent of popular music and jazz subtly laces
through this music. <u>Prelude</u> could be labelled neo-
romantic, <u>Toccata</u> neo-classic. <u>Prelude</u> has moderately ornate lyrical melody; as prominent is full acc
of added-note, doubly inflected, and chromatic chords.
Faster middle portion has single line in treble with
LH four-tone chords changing gradually by chromatic
motion. <u>Toccata</u> has fascinating variety. Hands may
alternate in one-line music; texture shifts to melody
accompanied by chords progressing irregularly. Full
treble triads enter with sudden dynamic change. Short
ostinatos emerge, including one related to boogie pattern. Animated rhythms have changing meters, ever
new patterns, and syncopations. Chromatic lines
thread through the constant motion. Climaxes well
prepared and maintained. (Leeds-NY, 1950, 9 pp.)
5 min, 10 sec.

7.89 SYDEMAN, WILLIAM. <u>Two Pieces for Piano.</u>
Sophisticated, witty, and playable. Melodies have
many leaps. Rhythms and meters shift constantly.
Texture is generally thin. Atonal. I is ABA; A is
slow (quasi dance) and B is fast. B is very loud,
contrasting furious single-note flurries with chordal
stabs. Moderately fast II has few notes; rests separate brief activity. (In 5.3, 4 pp.) MM.

7.90 TCHEREPNIN, ALEXANDER. Polka.
Blithe novelty number with sure audience appeal.
Chromatic added-note or doubly inflected chords, often
moving parallel, are superimposed on obvious tonal
harmonies. Rapid finger and hand staccato broken
chords, LH broken tenths and rapid back-and-forth
motion. Always four-measure phrases. Conservative.
(Tem, 1954, 3 pp.) MM.

7.91 TOMASI, HENRI. Berceuse.
Fanciful. Alternates in an improvisatory manner between recitativelike single line fragments and polytonal
fragments sounding like nursery tune played by bells.
Excellent practice in discovering simple musical content amid complicated-looking (not complicated to play)
writing. Translations are "simple but expressive," and
"very much surrounded, drowned (like distant bells)"
(p 1), "fairylike" (p 2), and "transient" (p 3). (Led,
1959, 3 pp.) MM.

7.92 VLAD, ROMAN. Studi Dodecafonici (1943--rev 1957).
Dodecaphonic Studies are romantic and expansively expressive. Same tone set used throughout; set includes
two minor triads, a fourth and a fifth, which lead un-
derstandably to tonal impressions. Flexible piano textures and moderately wide range. Conservative rhythm.
III is a Presto "figured variation after Study I;" melody from I is imbedded in rapid broken chords, motion frequently progressing hand over hand up and
down the keyboard. Translation (p 8) is "All of the
dynamic markings, from this point on, refer to the
tones already found in Study I. The 32nd notes must
be softer." III leads attacca to IV, an intensely expressive Andantino. On last page composer refers to
Chopin's Prelude in b by means of repeated tones and
bass upward motion arpeggio. (Zer, 1958, 15 pp.)
4 pieces. 12 min. Ped.

7.93 WEBER, BEN. Humoreske, Op. 49.
"Delicato" describes refined appeal. Twelve-tone.
Repetitions always varied. Motive of two repeated
short tones. Basically three voices, although harmony
nearly as important as polyphony. Composer requests
pedal use only in few indicated places. (In 6.4, 4 pp.)
Some Ped.

7.94 WEBERN, ANTON. Klavierstück (1925).
Piano Piece, by one of most important composers of
our time, is "in the tempo of a minuet." Strict
twelve-tone writing, with only a few irregularities.
Numerous melodic and harmonic major sevenths and
minor ninths. Extraordinary emphasis on single tones,
because range is so varied and because each tone has
its separate dynamic. Some four against three
rhythms. A few fast leaps. (UE 13490, 1966, 2 pp
--also in 8.3.)

7.95 WEISGALL, HUGO. Two Improvisations (1964, 1966).
Subtitled Graven Images No. 6, these are twelve-tone
works for the very discerning. Lyrical and sensitive
I is marked "freely flowing and flexible." Beat con-
sciousness blurred by long tones beginning in middle
of eighth notes, but rhythm not really difficult. Main
melody in treble. Texture is moderately full. While
second and seventh emphasis in I continues in II, fifths
also frequent. The Allegro, marked Molto marcato,
is often ff. Each hand often has double or triple notes.
In grazioso measures texture thinned to two voices.
(Pr, 1968, 4 pp.) MM.

7.96 WIRÉN, DAG. Sonatin, Op. 25 (1950).
Connected movements possess fine pianistic flair.
Many legato and staccato thirds in first and last movements. Masterful composition undergirds pleasantly
facile tonal work. Irrepressible motor motion in the
Allegro moderato. First idea in G lydian mode. In
second compelling idea RH has leaps in thirds over an
octave ostinato. In sonata form, minus development
and recapitulation of second idea. Impassive, "neu-
tral" series of common chords serve as chaconne pattern for the Andante--progression has been used for
bridge in first movement. In the merry closing Allegro prominent minor third upbeat comes from first
movement. After perpetual motion builds to fff bitonal
climax, first idea, never escaping the minor third,
serves as subject of an amusing fugato. Ending is
simplest scale over dominant to tonic progression. (In
6.5, 8 pp.) 3 movements. 7, some 5.

LEVEL 8

8.1 Canadian Composers, Fourteen Piano Pieces By.
Fast numbers and those with wit are particularly appealing. Ten pieces considered worthy of review, a high percentage. (See 3.23, 3.29, 4.84, 5.15, 5.103, 6.111, 7.21, 8.15, 8.27, and 8.89.) Seven are selections from larger works. More music than average on each page. Chosen for Canadian League of Composers by pianists and teachers Roubakine, Kilburn, and Moss. Foreword, biographies, and factual material on music in English and French. Contains music by Beckwith, Betts, Blackburn, Brott, Coulthard, Dolin, Fleming, Freedman, Kasemets, Morawetz, Morel, Papineau-Couture, Somers, and Weinzweig. (Har, 1955, 33 pp.) 16 pieces, 14 composers. Some Fngr, MM & Ped. 8, some 3, 4, 5, 6 & 7.

8.2 DESCAVES, LUCETTE, ed. Les Nouveaux Contemporains (Premier recueil).
All pieces in the New Contemporaries, first collection, are attractive and most are easily accessible. Idiomatic writing for the piano. Progressive in difficulty. Admirable editing. Six works contemporary enough to be included. (See 5.79, 5.126, 6.36, 8.6, 8.58 and 8.86.) Titles in French. Contains music by Alain, Aubin, Bitsch, Chailley, Dutilleux, Lesur, Noël-Gallon, Revel, Roizenblat, Sauguet, Thiriet, and Tomasi. (Chou, 1965, 43 pp.) 12 pieces, 12 composers. Fngr, MM & Ped. 8, some 5 & 6.

8.3 Styles in 20th-Century Piano Music.
Splendid collection. Revised and extended since first published in 1951. "Composers from 14 countries are represented." Comments in German and English. Much music printed on each page. Ten of the twelve works first published since 1950 are reviewed. (See 5.153, 6.117, 6.149, 7.48, 7.94, 8.38, 8.39, 8.70

and 8.82.) Contains works by Apostel, Bartók, Bennett, Blacher, Boulez, Burkhard, Casella, von Einem, Hába, Haubenstock-Ramati, Hauer, Jelinek, Kodály, Krenek, Martin, Milhaud, Paccagnini, Petyrek, Poot, Pousseur, Reger, Schoenberg, Skalkottas, Stockhausen, Strauss, Szymanowski, Tcherepnin, Wagner-Régeny, Webern, Wellesz and Wladigeroff.   (UE 12050E, 1968, 89 pp.) 35 pieces, 31 composers. One-half have MM, some Ped. Anal, Biog. 8, some 5, 6 & 7.

8.4   36 Twentieth-Century Piano Pieces.
In this useful collection four works were first published since 1950 and are reviewed. (See 7.67, 8.7 and 8.11.) Contains music by Antheil, Barber, Bartók, Bernstein, Bloch, Carpenter, Chávez, Creston, Debussy, Dello Joio, Fauré, Fine, Grainger, Griffes, Kabalevsky, Khachaturian, Krenek, MacDowell, Muczynski, Prokofieff, Rachmaninoff, Ravel, Schuman, Scott, Shostakovitch, and Tcherepnin. (GS, nd, 197 pp.) 36 pieces, 26 composers. Some Fngr, MM & Ped.   8, some 5 & 7.

8.5   ABSIL, JEAN. Passacaille, Op. 101, 1959.
Neo-romantic work of admirable construction and expressive variety.   Traditional, full piano figurations like arpeggios, rapid chord displacements, broken and harmonic octaves, etc. Passacaglia bass uses all twelve tones in a symmetrical order in twenty numbered sections.   French comments explain that ostinato alternates with its inversion; both shapes used in retrograde in slower sections ten through thirteen.   Chromatic tonal harmony includes many tritones, also diminished chords.   (CBDM, 1966, 9 pp.)   10 min. Anal.

8.6   ALAIN, OLIVIER. Intermezzo.
Luxuriantly chromatic tonal music.   Full rich texture shown by chords as large as thirteenths, final chord (for example) with added second, fourth, and seventh, and use of three staves. Many double and triple notes, sometimes moving parallel; fingering such as five over four for legato.   Largo 12/8 includes many sixteenths and a few thirty-seconds; some polyrhythms like four against three.   While primarily p, builds to ff climax. Requires ninth reach. (In 8.2, 4 pp.) Fngr, MM, Ped.

8.7 ANTHEIL, GEORGE. Toccata No. 2 (1948).
Will bring down the house with raucous reminders of
American folk music. Out-of-key harmonies and polyharmonies heard against obvious tonality. Two basic
melodies are usually fragmented; brash surroundings,
where hands often alternate, are equally noticeable.
Splendid practice for chords, octaves, leaps, bravura,
and endurance. Hearty climaxes emphasized by surrounding softer dynamics and less pedaling. (GS,
1951, 6 pp--also in 8.4.) MM, some Ped.

8.8 APOSTEL, HANS ERICH. Klavierstück, Op. 8.
Wagner's Tristan is surely the expressive and musical ancestor of this intense Molto lento Piano Piece.
Numerous contrapuntal chromatic strands. Constantly
shifting tonalities in harmonically dense, chromatic
idiom. Motivic and formal repetitions. Much rubato.
(Dob, 1964, 5 pp.)

8.9 BACEWICZ, GRAŻYNA. II Sonata (1953).
Full texture work has pianistic bravado with many effective climaxes. Both tertial and quartal chromatic
tonal harmony. Agitato first movement in sonata form
is fascinatingly varied. Rich sounds come from chromatic parallel first inversion chords. Texture sometimes thinned to quick alternating hands scampering up
and down the keyboard in one-line music; bold few-
note melodies also filled in by obvious keyboard figurations. Strong bass octaves. Remote Largo tranquillo,
opening and closing over ostinatos of two seventh or
ninth chords, builds twice to impressive climaxes.
Fugato section is warmly expressive. Brilliant Vivo
Toccata is musically obvious. Streams of parallel
fourths, thirds, and first inversion chords alternating
between the hands and satirical dancelike melodies are
among the ingredients. Much bass register. (PWM,
1955, 19 pp.) 3 movements. 14 min. MM, some
Ped. 8, some 7.

8.10 BACEWICZ, GRAŻYNA. 10 Etudes (1957).
Nothing standard about these character pieces. Five
have something puckish about them; only two are slow.
Keyboard figurations, often almost unique, are consistent in each Etude; five Etudes use approximately
parallel construction for each hand. High dissonance
level; logical execution of figuration takes precedence
over harmonic niceties or facile appeal. Very broad-

ly tonal; sometimes polyharmonies. Forms carefully
controlled. Vivace II possesses gay, quick wit.
Brief ideas dissolve into short chromatic scales.
Broken triads in one hand often move contrary to motion in other hand. Quick passage work may stop for
chords alternating between hands. Wide range used.
III is an Allegretto hand staccato chord study of rondo
spirit. Many polyharmonic triads, which settle in G
and B at end. Much chromatic motion. Dynamics
never exceed f. MM seems too slow. Gentle VIII has
delicate broken-chord play colored by fourth and polychords. Melody and pedal tones change slowly amid
continual moderate speed, sixteenth note motion. Rapid motor motion never stops in X. Slurred broken
seconds, sevenths, and ninths alternating between hands
create intense mood. Short thumb melodies and a few
regularly spaced accents surface irregularly. Some
extensions. (PWM, 1958, 38 pp.) MM. 8, some 6
& 7.

8.11 BARBER, SAMUEL. Nocturne (Homage to John Field),
        Op. 33.
Warmly expressive number combines A-flat tonality in
acc with twelve-tone RH melody. (See article in The
Piano Quarterly for Summer, 1970.) Pianistic style
related to Field and Chopin. Highly ornamented lyrical melody changes at times from single notes to repeated double notes, descending thirds or octaves;
breaks into cadenza after middle section. Usually LH
has traditional extended broken chords. Imitation in
middle section. (GS, 1959, 4 pp--also in 8.4.) MM.

8.12 BERGMAN, ERIK. Sonatin (1950), Op. 36.
Compelling logic and strong drama present. All three
movements, particularly first and last, based on three
three-tone opening chords which include perfect and
augmented fourths. Forms evolve in no set patterns.
Atonal and dissonant. Varied pianistic requirements.
First movement clearly states unifying three chords
and immediately moves to a Poco animato e ritmico.
Hands usually alternate, using one-line passage work
and chords. Builds to fff ending. Flexible rhythms
have beat division by two through six, including declamatory short-long values. Sostenuto e fantastico includes a recitative passage with a few broken triads.
Poco presto e risoluto finale uses intervals from motto
chords in a melody of strong profile; rapid step-wise

motion in acc.   Prominent mirror motion, hands ex-
changing roles.   Builds to furioso, maestoso procla-
mation of main idea in octaves with simultaneous original and mirror order.   (In 6.5, 10 pp.) 3 movements. 6 min. Biog. 8, some 6.

8.13 BERKOWITZ, SAUL. Syncopations, 1958.
Combines irrepressible jazz mood and admirable compositional skill.   Syncopations involve anticipations of
both quarter and third of a beat; numerous dotted and
triplet rhythms in "moderately fast" work.   In 4/4
meter, piece has perpetual motion boogie ostinato of
two and two-thirds beats.   There are also other subtly
varied repetitions.   At crucial points key is A-flat;
elsewhere A is identifiable.   Pedal points often anchor
harmony.   Frequent parallel seconds.   Moderately full
texture. (In 6.4, 4 pp.) MM.

8.14 BOZAY, ATTILA. Variazioni, Op. 10 (1964).
Ten Variations of decided character and variety.
Many directions in Italian hint at expressive range.
Theme, marked "like a popular Hungarian Song," uses
the four transformations of a twelve-tone set.   In some
variations theme is missing and title seems to be used
in the general sense that twelve-tone technique is a
continuous variation.   Complete pianism required with
fleet figures, fast repeated tones, leaps and hand exchanges, cluster chords, trills, etc.   (EMB, 1968,
12 pp.) 9 min. MM, Ped.

8.15 BROTT, ALEXANDER. Sacrilege (1941).
Take Bach's Two-part Invention in F, substitute c-
sharp for the first c, f-sharp for the next f, allow
two measures for two extra ideas in the subject (each
developed separately), and the result is an amusing
spoof.   Excitement provided by offbeat harmonic minor
seconds, syncopated accents, chromatically moving sequences in contrary motion, written-in accelerations,
etc.   Splendid for finger staccato, hand independence,
and general entertainment.   (In 8.1, 4 pp.) Biog.

8.16 BRUNSWICK, MARK. Six Bagatelles (1958).
Sensitive works require flexible interpretation and
awareness of line.   Largely non-tonal harmony; some
suggestion of tonality.   Except for acc details no material is repeated or traditional.   Four Bagatelles are
fast.   Rapid repeated double notes of Fourth and Sixth

Bagatelles are greatest technical difficulty. Included
also are very fast scales and arpeggios. Material in
II alternates between chordal gestures and a dolce melody accompanied by enticing thirds. Lento III suggests
D because of RH tremolo thirds on D and final bass
tones; also some hint of polytonality. Baritone register lyrical melody. Allegro scherzando V has dolce
wide-span lines with brief faster flurries. Essentially in two voices. (In 6.4, 6 pp.) MM. 8, some 6
& 7.

8.17 CASTILLO, MANUEL. Preludio, Diferencias y Toc-
     cata (1959).
    Prelude, Variations and Toccata is bold-gestured mu-
sic of strong emotional impact. First theme from
Albeniz's El Puerto in the Iberia Suite is used with
imagination. Frequent parallel added-note, cluster,
and fourth chords. Pianistically idiomatic work won
a national prize in 1959. Several misprints should be
fairly apparent. Prelude uses first few tones of theme
as a freely shifting ground bass, sometimes as part of
ff polychords, sometimes in imitation, sometimes in
inner voice with surrounding acc; texture also shifts
freely. Expressive intent varies from the declamatory
to an improvisatory, impressionistic section in which
beat divisions by two, three, and four occur. In the
Variations the phrygian, Albeniz theme is first stated
completely without acc, then used very freely in fourteen variations. Pianistic variety includes parallel
chord streams, octaves, ostinato of added-note chords,
rapid coupled writing, and quick hand alternations.
Brilliant Toccata uses repeated tone element of theme
in many guises. Dissonant linear counterpoint often
present, one element usually chords. Rising chromatic passages build excitement to a dramatic peak.
(UME, 1962, 24 pp.) MM.

8.18 CORTÉS, RAMIRO. Suite for Piano (1955).
    Vigorous music of strong profile. Percussive and dis-
sonant harmonies. Many meter changes and irregular
accents. Effective piano writing. Tenth reach. In
the Stravinsky-influenced Maestoso Sinfonia a preten-
tious chordal passage frames an inventive, eloquent,
and wide-range grazioso central section. Widely-
spaced chordal passages include reiterated tonic chord
tones and determined dissonant inner voice leadings.
LH has many lateral shifts. Original Lento Arioso

Sentimentale is played "always with exaggerated senti-
mentality." RH texture alone is complex: a single
melody line, decorated with exotic ornaments, is further filled out by chromatic acc; then the melody is
lost in exuberant double notes. In f, with many accidentals. Slashing Allegro molto Finale is marked
"barbaro." Passages are labelled "in the manner of
ragtime." (EV, 1957, 13 pp.) 4 movements. MM,
some Ped. 8, some 7.

8.19 COULTHARD, JEAN. Prelude No. 1, Leggiero.
Masterfully constructed miniature of gentle mien. Neo-
romantic music has moderately fast RH passage work
of minor thirds and seconds pivoting around the thumb;
rhythms include seven against three. Shifts to Meno
mosso, very chromatic material. (BMI, 1959, 2 pp.)
MM.

8.20 DALLAPICCOLA, LUIGI. Quaderno Musicale di An-
      nalibera.
Musical Notebook for Annalibera is a rigorously concentrated work in classic twelve-tone technique. Makes
little concession to easy accessibility--performer must
have interpretative maturity. Three of the eleven sections are canons. 3 gives all four versions of the set
and indicates a different dynamic level for each voice.
5 is a two-voice canon in contrary motion a half beat
apart; 7 is a retrograde canon with four versions of
the set making up "a rhythmically subtle two-part
theme." (Musical Quarterly, Jan. 1955.) 1, in homage to Bach, uses the B A C H motive. 2 and 8 have
coarseness; 6 and 11 are lyrical. Rhythms only moderately difficult, although 6 has a measure in 7/8 in
which one hand has two, three, and two while the other
divides three beats by four and four beats by three.
Many directions in Italian. (Zer, 1953, 15 pp.) 14
min. MM.

8.21 DAVID, JOSÉ. Le Marais et Ses Moulins (Impres-
      sions de Vendée).
The Swamp and Its Mills (Impressions from Vendée)
is pleasant, facile "Scherzando, vif" in French tradition. Chromatic harmonies and numerous modulations
label the work conservative; also has momentary polychords and chords with double inflections. Numerous
attractive ideas follow one another with little repetition. Wide keyboard and technique explorations include

arpeggios, hand staccato double notes, and full chords.
Fine practice for reading accidentals. (Dur, 1952, 8
pp.) MM, some Ped.

8.22 DELLO JOIO, NORMAN. Nocturne in F-Sharp Minor.
Wonderfully fanciful. Interestingly busy, covering wide
keyboard range. Uses wide reach. Middle sections
in e-flat and c-sharp have cakewalk rhythm and ornate
wide-leaping melody. Freely uses all twelve tones.
(CF, 1950, 5 pp.)

8.23 DE MEESTER, LOUIS. Petite Suite.
Little Suite is quite accessible twelve tone writing.
Same symmetrical set with several thirds used through-
out. Unordered segments found. Some repetition; one
ostinato used. Rhythmically traditional. I is graceful
Moderato of moderately wide range. III is a Lento of
even tread. While LH usually has quarter note motion,
RH shows some evidence of progressive diminution.
Original and retrograde transformations of set used to-
gether; frequent seventh leaps. IV, a playful Scher-
zando, is pointillistic; some isolated dynamic markings.
Tone clusters present, sometimes gradually built up.
(Metr, 1956, 8 pp.) 5 movements. MM, some Ped.
8, some 6 & 7.

8.24 FOSS, LUKAS. Scherzo Ricercato (1953).
Presto energetic, tonal work certain to please if given
crisp, accurate performance. Momentary dissonances
result from contrapuntal motion. Admirable economy
of material. Rollicking 6/8 rhythms need split-second
metrical timing because of cross accents, stops on last
third of beats, and rests on following main beats. Requires finger strength. "This étude in 18th century
contrapuntal devices, with emphasis on their play and
humor, was composed for the Young Pianists Competition sponsored by the Wichita Falls Symphony, 1953."
Admirable economy of material, in general form of
scherzo, ricercato, (ricercare) scherzo and ricercato,
the last ricercato including features of the scherzo.
Scherzo has octaves, quick hand alternation, RH two-
voice composition needing strong individual fingers,
and octave or third coupling. In ricercato sections
the subject, in a constant quarter-eighth rhythm, is
doubled by octave, imitated, anticipated or delayed an
eighth, and inverted; original and inverted orders also appear at same time. Soft legato ricercato is as

spontaneous as scherzo. (CF, 1961, 10 pp.) 4 min.
MM, some Ped.

8.25 FRAENKEL, WOLFGANG. Variationen und Fantasien
     (1954).
     Variations and Fantasies written in intensely expres-
     sive, atonal, chromatic idiom of Schoenberg: his Op.
     19, No. 3, used in its entirety as theme. In general,
     only motives are used in the variations, although first
     five retain same measure length as Schoenberg's minia-
     ture. Three longer Fantasies are spaced between ten
     shorter Variations. First Fantasy is three-voice
     fugue, followed by scherzolike Variations. Last Fan-
     tasy is passacaglia using Schoenberg's bass more com-
     pletely than elsewhere. Theme restated at end. Slow-
     er numbers have much polyphony. Complete pianistic
     technique required, from a warmly singing tone to rap-
     id finger work. (UE 12549, 1959, 23 pp.) 15 min.

8.26 FRANÇAIX, JEAN. Eloge de la Danse (1947).
     How well these works In Praise of the Dance capture
     a flirtatious waltz spirit! Elusiveness of music aptly
     matches that of the quotations of Valery in French--
     translations below are incomplete. Sophisticated chro-
     matic tonal harmonies, melodies often even more chro-
     matic. Usually soft dynamics suggest subtle interpre-
     tations needed. Traditional acc patterns. II ("... she
     was ... yes and no ...") has the skeleton of a waltz,
     with rests on many beats. Three-unit patterns fre-
     quently spread across two measures; also two equal-
     length melody tones in each measure. IV ("... the
     facility of her whole body ...") is Vivo tour de force
     because RH combines five-finger chromatic ascents or
     descents in pp perpetual motion melody. No thumb un-
     der. VI ("... moved by the breezes of music") in-
     cludes stronger fiber of diatonic writing than else-
     where, providing greater brilliance, although in the
     end elegant soft moods of chromaticism prevail. Nu-
     merous double and triple notes. (ScS 4016, 1950, 18
     pp.) 6 pieces. Some Fngr & Ped. 8, some 6.

8.27 FREEDMAN, HARRY. Scherzo (1950).
     Witty music, marked "very rhythmically but lightly,"
     bounces along by two and three-note slurs. Essential-
     ly in two voices moving at the same time generally in
     contrary motion, both slurred alike. 7/8, 6/8, 2/4
     and 3/4 meters. Music levels out to repeated longer

chords. Middle section more flowing. Broadly tonal,
all twelve tones freely used. (In 8.1, 2 pp.) MM.

8.28 FRICKER, P. RACINE. Twelve Studies, Op. 38.
Works of integrity and originality. Interest comes
from sturdy pursuit of logical ideas; usual "charm"
not considered. All but two of the atonal works unified by plans indicated in subtitles, such as (a) canonic
by inversion and augmentation, (b) accelerando and ri-
tardando, (c) for the right hand only, and (d) toccata
(minor seconds and fourths). Varied technical requirements equal for each hand. Lento: liberamente 1
(mirror-chords) has craggy strength. Cluster elements
in first three fingers (extension between third and fifth
fingers) are dissonant; octaves bring change in middle
section. Lento 3 (cantabile for left hand) has fascinating textures. LH melody, which constantly evolves,
ranges more than three octaves while acc uses a quick
short passage and exactly articulated tones and chords.
Much RH over LH. 7 (thirds) uses its interval in
smooth legato manner, usually in RH. Moderato study
has gentle appeal not pursued in most works of the collection. 11 (legato and staccato) is a charming Allegretto again, with fascinating texture. Usually a close
range legato melody alternates between hands; when
each hand has melody tone, it has simultaneously a
staccato acc tone in outer fingers. Considerable fantasy and brilliance in Pomposo 12 (octaves). Octaves
are used in both hands in patterns, yet with variety:
hands alternating and together, in imitation, and RH
legato while LH is staccato. (Scho 10804, 1962, 34
pp.) 23 min. Some Ped. 8, some 7.

8.29 GENZMER, HARALD. Capriccio (2 Sonatine) (1950).
Neo-classic work showing Hindemith influences. Useful for developing agility; three movements are fast.
Even the transition ideas have character. Tonal, with
free use of all twelve tones; some modal influences.
No key signatures. Much finger or hand non-legato or
staccato contributes to capricious quality. Allegro is
in clear sonata form with constant development; recapitulation much changed from exposition. Usually in
two-part texture of lively, traditional rhythmic interest. Presto Scherzo in binary form with wide ranging
single-line staccatos. Transparently clear writing.
Lovely Tranquillo III has three types of material:
warm double or triple notes in each hand moving in

contrary motion, flexible coupled writing, and fast
treble scales. IV is a unified Allegro moderato.
Rhythms restless because of syncopations and patterns
against the meter. Textures include repeated tone acc
and dissonant imitative counterpoint. RH has rapid
arpeggios. (Scho 4288, 1954, 10 pp.) Four movements. Some Fngr, MM. 8, some 7.

8.30 GINASTERA, ALBERTO. Rondo on Argentine Chil-
    dren's Folk Tunes (1947).
Wonderfully skillful and witty, ideal for an encore.
Allegro melody alternates with two slower ones. Composer's fanciful settings keep naive spirit of tunes.
Tunes often accompanied by counter chromatic line over
a pedal, or by two alternating triads. Diatonic melodies may have wandering tonal harmonizations adding
up to polyharmony; g melody may be harmonized as if
it were in mixolydian mode. Pianistic variety includes
singing melodies, rapid parallel chords, and RH finger
staccato. (Barry, 1951, 4 pp.) MM.

8.31 GINASTERA, ALBERTO. Suite de Danzas Criollas.
Suite of Native Dances is an inevitable success with
audiences; primitive brilliance contrasts with bewitching moods. Brilliance requires handling full chordal
textures with some skips and endurance with octaves
and chords. Sultry atmospheres using long pedals
need subtle balancing of sonorities. Each movement
moves attacca to the next. Tonal harmonies; polyharmonies and cluster chords bring color. Numerous
polyrhythms. Melody in "calm and poetic" IV is
coupled by octaves and thirds; acc has broken chord
grace notes and extended rolled chords. Numerous
short-long rhythms. In a, with frequent exotic chromatic changes in melody. Marvellous full texture variety in Scherzando V. Simple scale or chordal melodies appear with ostinato acc, coupled by fourths or
fifths, tripled by octaves, etc. Melody may be omitted, giving way to slashing added-note chords with
simultaneous or alternating 3/4 and 6/8. Smashing
Coda (3 pp) is a Presto ed energico. Many meter and
register changes. Resourceful brash sonorities always
ff or more. (Barry, 1957, 12 pp.) 6 movements.
MM, some Ped. 8, some 5 & 6.

8.32 GOOSENS, EUGENE. Capriccio.
Delightful novelty number, based on composer's Hurdy

Gurdy Man from Kaleidoscope, contains "nostalgic"
non-harmonic tones, chromaticisms, and numerous
modulations.   Short scherzando and con energico episodes are part of constantly shifting moods.   Splendid
for developing effervescent performing style with numerous tempo and dynamic changes.   Fine chord study;
numerous thirds.   No key signature, but many sharps
and flats.   (Ches, 1960, 3 pp.)   MM, some Ped.

8.33   GUARNIERI, M. CAMARGO.   Valsas (1-5).
Five Waltzes have neo-romantic melodic and harmonic
grace; also linear interest.   Lyrical melodies constantly unfold.   Principal melody almost always in upper
treble; clearly marked secondary melodies often alternate between hands.   Very chromatic melodies and harmonies over clear tonal basis.   All main keys are
minor, no key signatures; many accidentals.   Full textures are significant feature.   Rhythms usually traditional.   Forms always ABA.   Few brief fortissimos.
Printing could be clearer.   All are conservative.   Second Waltz, marked "lazily," usually has a binding line
of direct chromaticism in one of the melodies.   Form
is ABA, with repetition of A fuller--unusual for collection.   In c-sharp, with C harmonies on final extended
tonic chord suggesting luxuriant harmonies.   Fifth
Waltz is fanciful and spontaneous.   A little thinner in
texture than most, section A having no counter melody
beyond a chromatic bass line.   Some measures shift to
duple meter and have four against three rhythms.
(Ric-Br, 1962, 26 pp.)   Some Fngr, MM. 8, some 7.

8.34   HALFFTER, RODOLFO.   Second Piano Sonata.
While not profound, content of this work is facile and
attractive.   Piano textures are skillful and usually traditional; wide keyboard range.   Clear tonal harmonies,
often moving in parallel motion, may slip momentarily
into polyharmony.   Common chords sometimes uncom-
monly juxtaposed; some performers may find this and
transition techniques too obvious.   Opening Allegro is
unpretentiously neo-classic.   Form bears resemblance
to sonata form; recapitulation of first theme mostly de-
voted to development of first motive--includes many
modulations.   Numerous accompanying parallel sevenths.
Meter changes, and slurring contrary to meter.
Jaunty Rondo, always in C, is heard four times: parallel fifths dissolve into rapid passage work, fifths are
broken, and meter shifts from 3/4 to 3/8.   Closes

with bold chordal shifts between A-flat, B, and tonic
C.   Earlier, main episode's treble is notated in A-
flat and bass in E.   (PAU, 1955, 33 pp.)   4 movements.   MM, some Ped.   Biog.

8.35 HALFFTER, RODOLFO.   Tercera Sonata, Op. 30.
Third Sonata is very modern although not complex.
Mechanistic, economical twelve-tone music, with repetitions of material, sometimes immediately at a new
octave level, or changed a half step.   Material is
sometimes inverted, or in reversed hands.   Throughout, rests separate short ideas.   Each hand has lateral and hand-over-hand motion.   In the opening Allegro
fantasy emerges from the planned construction.   Motion often stopped by fermatas.   Meters, changing
from 5/16 to 3/8 to 2/4, etc., are not difficult when
basic beat is secure.   RH has rapid, repeated double
and triple notes.   Graceful Moderato cantabile is clear
in form with two statements of main material and a
coda.   Foreword in Spanish gives directions for playing
some indeterminate passages in slow movement.   Study
in sonority provided by wide ranges of economical material.   Impetuoso movement, like the first, also stops
often and has rapid RH repeated figure.   Many thirds.
(EMM, 1968, 20 pp.)   4 movements.   Some Ped.   8,
some 7.

8.36 HAMILTON, IAIN.   Nocturnes with Cadenzas (1963).
Sensitive timbre explorations throughout, with varied
pedaling.   Extreme ranges.   Unusual form with four
Nocturnes separated by three Cadenzas.   Each moves
attacca to next, although barring of last Cadenza and
Nocturne may suggest possibility of performing them
alone.   Nocturnes are slow, Cadenzas fast.   Dynamics
soft except for two numbers.   Numerous cluster chords,
sometimes requiring unusual fingering and accurate
leaps.   Pliable rhythms need counting; most difficult
is half beat divided simultaneously by five and three.
Usually legato.   Tenth reach used.   Cadenzas not
barred.   Cadenzas I and III quickly alternate hands on
a single line; same tone set used in a free manner.
Nocturne II marked "calm; hesitating."   (Scho 10882,
1968, 11 pp.)   MM, some Ped.

8.37 HARRIS, ROY.   Toccata.
Tremendously vital work successfully combines early
American features of dance and hymn, as well as tra-

ditional toccata and fugue styles. These elements,
along with an opening five-note motto of melodic fourths
and fifths, are convincingly welded together. Much
coupled writing, usually two octaves apart. Fuller texture aided by frequent use of sostenuto pedal to sustain
chordal interruptions--pedal indications unusually complete. Continual rhythmic interest from irregular accents, meter changes, varied articulation, slurring,
and pace. Tonal work uses all twelve tones. Harmony of hymn episode influenced by combined tertial
and quartal chords and by some polychords. Two-
voice fugue using motto is skillfully introduced following hymn-influenced material. After long dominant
pedal the toccata style, including declamatory chords,
returns. Work belongs to Sigma Alpha Iota modern
music series. (CF, 1950, 10 pp.) Ped, MM.

8.38 HAUBENSTOCK-RAMATI, ROMAN. Klavierstück
      (1965).
      Post-Webern Piano Piece with extreme pitches and
      frequently different dynamics for each sound. Barless
      music has numerous playing directions for unconven-
      tional notation. "The tempo results ... from the (var-
      iable) subjective perception of rest and unrest and from
      the interaction of both." (From Klavierstücke (I) UE
      14255.) (In 8.3, 2 pp.) *Anal, Biog.

8.39 HAUER, JOSEF MATTHIAS. XXII Zwölftonspiel.
      XXII Twelve-Tone Play is useful etude-like work. Lat-
      eral motion emphasized with RH ascending arpeggios,
      a quick descent to begin again, and chord displace-
      ments; also varied extensions. Frequent chords with-
      out thirds. Beats divided by threes and fours are
      juxtaposed. No dynamic or tempo indications. MM
      must be about 90 each quarter. Not in strict twelve-
      tone technique. (In 8.3, 4 pp.) 7 min.

8.40 HELPS, ROBERT. Image.
      Image well describes ephemeral qualities of this po-
      etic lento rubato. Very obscurely tonal, A having
      some emphasis. Double inflections used. Repetition
      of descending melodic fourths and motives in measures
      one and six anchor the music to some extent. Explor-
      atory sonorities, including short low tones and upper
      tremolos, are sustained by fairly long pedals.
      Rhythms include triplets across two beats and four
      against three. (In 6.4, 2 pp.) Ped.

8.41 HELPS, ROBERT. Portrait.
Largo of distinct and varied profile. Of three types of
writing the first is most complex, appearing irregularly, sometimes strident and highly declamatory, sometimes softer. Warmly lyrical second material, in four
voices, appears twice, merging the first time into opening declamation. Third material is anchored by RH octave tremolo acc figure ranging over three octaves.
Full keyboard texture and much dynamic variety. Harmony is eclectic with double inflections, seventh and
fourth chords, etc. Ends in G-sharp, but with raised
fourth. (Pet 6997, 1966, 8 pp.) 6 min, 30 sec. MM,
Ped.

8.42 HERNANDEZ, MONCADA EDVARDO. Costeña.
Coastal Girl is an expressive work with insistent drive.
Uncomplicated, it sounds more difficult than it is. Irregularly accented perpetual motion rhythms bring an
earthy vigor; also polyrhythms of three and two. Triad harmonies heighten primitive feeling; percussive
polyharmonies also frequent. Harmonies often move by
seconds. Several short harmonic patterns repeated.
Tonal; some dorian mode. Equal hand emphasis; LH
has ascending arpeggios and other lateral motion. Develops brilliance. Publication aided by National Insti-
tute of Fine Arts and Mexican Society of Authors and
Composers. (EMM, 1962, 7 pp.) MM.

8.43 KOCH, ERLAND VON. Sonatina No. 2, Op. 46 (1950).
Admirably idiomatic piano writing, with hands treated
equally. Outer two movements are gaily extrovert,
middle is hauntingly beautiful. Foreword reveals composer's admiration for Mozart, which shows in tightly
constructed movements. Allegro vivace has both rapid scales and less rapid repeated chords. Modal, legato double-note ostinato acc for second theme. Moderately exotic, lyrical Adagio meanders chromatically.
In c-sharp. Fine tone study. Final Allegro molto has
numerous fourths and fifths, partially in ostinato acc.
Pianistic variety includes hand staccatos, scales, double
and triple notes, quick hand alternation, and some
lyricism. (In 6.5, 9 pp.) 3 movements. MM, Ped.
Biog. 8, some 6.

8.44 KOHN, KARL. Five Bagatelles (1961).
Exquisite works, predominantly of a scherzo nature,
use contemporary techniques like atonalism and moder-

ate pointillism. Repetitions and other patterns help
communication. Very careful editing. Allegro moderato I has distinct gestures, often of short duration,
ending sforzando or staccato. Some mirror writing.
Detailed dynamics and frequent rests. Usually legato
lento IV has gentle, piquant chord sonorities. Medium
wide range. Spontaneous bounce of Allegro vivace V
due to staccato leaps and two-note slurs. Many melodic and harmonic sevenths and ninths, also thirds,
sixths and fifths. (CF, 1967, 9 pp.) MM, Ped. 8,
some 6 & 7.

8.45 KRAFT, LEO. Allegro Giocoso (1957).
Energetically brash, yet also gentle. Balance between
finger work and chords. Tonal progressions often gov-
erned by polyharmony blocks treated as two contrapuntal lines; also many ninth chords. Lively rhythms
have freely changing unmetered measures, polyrhythms
with clear notation and varied, cross slurrings. Full
keyboard range. (In 6.4, 5 pp.)

8.46 LACERDA, OSVALDO. Baião (da Suite No. 1) (1961).
Arresting combination of attractive melody, familiar
tango rhythms, and striking harmonic acc. Main melody in pure mixolydian mode on D-flat. Title, defined
as "rock and roll type of music and dance," not really
applicable to this "playful" music. Opening ostinato
harmonization is based on G (with polymodality important throughout), while others have a D-flat tonic, dominant or subdominant pedal. Phrygian mode on b-flat
also used. "Without pedal" is direction; as texture
thickens, particularly with two voices frequently in one
hand, legato fingering must be resourceful. (IVi,
1965, 6 pp.) MM, some Ped.

8.47 LACERDA, OSVALDO. Chôro (da Suite No. 1) (1961).
Appealing piece marked "nervous, but not too fast."
A Choro is based on "tunes played at popular festivals."
Intriguing combination of familiar elements. Clear tonal traits surrounded by many non-harmonic tones. Moderately contemporary. Many modulations. In melody/
acc texture, with acc frequently a syncopated counter
melody; acc also has irregular broken chords, often of
augmented and perfect fourths. "Without pedal" legato
acc requires careful fingering. Splendid study in simultaneous finger staccato with short slurs for melody and
legato for acc. Equal hand emphasis. (IVi, 1965, 4
pp.) MM.

8.48 LEDUC, JACQUES. Contrastes.
High-spirited and effective music of great Contrasts
indeed. Accessible work, sounding more difficult than
it is. Molto ritmico beginning and end has much non-
legato or forearm staccato; more tranquil middle section uses alternating hands for scaler and arpeggio acc.
Ideas change very frequently; ff dissonant, marcato
and pp leggiero, molto dolce measures found. Non-
tonal: bass and treble often seem to ignore each other; no key remains stable longer than few measures.
Meter changes occur in many succeeding measures,
with eighth note constant. Amazingly varied piano
writing includes (a) well marked bass acc with contrasting treble rhythm, (b) rapid RH passage work and
ostinatolike slower-moving bass, (c) syncopated harmonic fourths, major sevenths, or octaves with continuous staccato motion in acc hand, (d) quick hand alternations using octaves, and (e) coupled writing. Required by Belgian National Music Competition for 1967.
(SF, 1967, 8 pp.) MM.

8.49 LEES, BENJAMIN. Three Preludes (1962).
Abstract play of tones clothed in effective dramatic
gestures. Splendid balance between rhapsodic richness
and repetitions. Very freely tonal, including unstruc-
tured harmonies over pedal tones; some polyharmony.
Wide ranging (three staves often used), fast coupled
writing and broken chords are among the many pianistic styles. "Maestoso" nature of I comes from gong-
like jabs of a wide sonority and rapid passage work.
Form is like a rondo, but all else is flexible. Fanciful rhythms with many meter shifts, such as 3/4 to
5/8 to 3/4; also beats with varied subdivisions move
between fours and sevens. II, marked Moderato, re-
lates to impressionism by many fragments and by atmospheric repeated-tone acc; however, dynamics are
louder. Opening "tranquillo" moves to agitato to a
cadenzalike climax of two-part coupled sixths over a
bass pedal. Last chord is A-flat, with raised second,
fourth, and seventh. (B&H, 1968, 18 pp.) MM.

8.50 LESSARD, JOHN. Perpetual Motion.
Fine study in sonority. Necessary transparency of
texture will depend upon skillful pedaling and suitable
balance; LH is constantly busy with a trill-like acc
using moderate extensions. Both hands may have constant sixteenth note motion. Last movement of Stra-

vinsky's <u>Symphony of Psalms</u> provides a prominent
motive as well as tonal harmonies which are seldom
resolved.   Some three against four rhythms.   Much
RH over LH.   (Jos, 1968, 7 pp.)

8.51   LESUR, DANIEL.   Trois Études (1962).
Three Etudes are pianistically resourceful; all qualify
for subtitle of the second, "Etude in Sonority."   Andante flessible (flexible) "Etude for Crossing the
Hands" is gentle and original.   Melody divided between
hands, and usually with broken chord acc.   Acc uses
many lateral shifts, as does, of course, the crossing
of hands.   Much treble register.   Non-tonal.   "Etude
in Sonority" is a Largo ma un poco andante e con
anima.   Opaque harmonies tend to be polychords.
Serious and consistent chordal study.   LH tenth reach
an advantage.   Numerous rhythms of two against three.
Skillful "Etude for the Tremolo" is marked "fast but
well measured."   Much rotary motion, with both hands
having constant sixteenth note tremolos simultaneously
between double or triple notes and thumbs.   In C, with
much parallel chord motion; some chords with double
inflections.   Medium dynamics.   (Dur, 1963, 11 pp.)
8 min.   MM.   8, some 7.

8.52   LINKE, NORBERT.   Polyrhythmika Nr. 1.
Complex work, eminently playable.   Intensely expressive and fantastically varied.   Interpretation, particularly rhythmic, is demanding.   Flexible rhythms, me-
ticulously notated, shift in beat subdivisions from two
to seven and nearly as much across two beats.   Tempo changes carefully programmed by metronome.   Full
texture and wide keyboard range.   Dissonant atonal
harmonies in Viennese-school tradition; two different
twelve-tone sets emerge once.   Direction (p 5) is "a
little more fluent."   (HG 555, 1966, 6 pp.)   MM,
some Ped.

8.53   LINKE, NORBERT.   Polyrhythmika Nr. 2.
Fascinating study in cells of sonorities, the result of
convincing logic.   Twelve-tone work begins with short
sections of single tones surrounded, according to the
mirror principle, by chromatic tones above and below.
Slow and fast tempos alternate, as do short sections
with and without pedal.   Little by little clusters grow
until a near-two octave span of white, then black keys
are slammed at the climax.   One example of rhythms

separates repeated groups of three tones by one beat,
then by three-fourths of a beat, and finally by one-
third of a beat. Fast flurries of single tones are
heard, but little melody, as such. (HG 568, 1966, 10
pp.) MM, some Ped.

8. 54 MIHALOVICI, MARCEL.   Trois Pièces Nocturnes, Op.
      63 (1948, 1951).
      Three Nocturnal Pieces are salon music of solid con-
      tent. Sophisticated chromatic tonal harmony, in which
      modulations and chromatic non-harmonic tones are so
      frequent that keys are always in flux or non-determin-
      able. Idiomatic for piano. Allegretto capriccioso Im-
      promptu is charming and graceful, fine for rubato
      practice.   First line directions are "hesitating" and
      "but without any rigor." Numerous double notes, also
      double inflections. Dream (II) is diaphonous and vague.
      "This piece is played pp from one end to the other."
      Splendid study for very fast unpatterned conjunct mo-
      tion in alternate hands. First and last bass tones in-
      dicate key is c. Thoroughly French Epilogue is sensu-
      ous but tasteful. Numerous falling thirds; several unre-
      solved dominant seventh chords. (Heu, 1952, 9 pp.)
      MM, some Ped. 8, some 7.

8. 55 MILANO, ROBERT.   Toccata.
      Smashing bravura. Content not profound, but substan-
      tial enough to gain maximum impact from minimum re-
      sources. Numerous tonic and dominant LH thrusts.
      Often reiterated RH added-note chords range widely.
      Dynamics often increase to ff climaxes, even ffff at the
      end. Prominent octaves, fourths, and fifths. (Beek,
      1963, 7 pp.) MM.

8. 56 MILHAUD, DARIUS.   Sonatine (1956).
      Skilled craftsmanship. Always interesting because of
      moderately aggressive modernisms. Flexible harmo-
      nies include quick key changes, momentary polyharmo-
      nies, freely associated triads, added-note chords and
      chromatically changed chords moving parallel. Through-
      out, moderately fast double and triple notes in each
      hand. In the opening Decidé moods are changed fre-
      quently by changes of dynamics and writing styles.
      Splendid variety of texture includes single note melody
      and chordal acc (often thirds), coupled writing, and tri-
      ads in each hand. Many ideas emerge and recede flu-
      idly. Melody of dignified Modéré requires clarity when

each hand has double and triple notes sometimes reach-
ing to a ninth. Moderate skips. Numerous rhythmic
and articulation details in the rapid Alerte (quick).
(EMT, 1956, 8 pp.) 3 movements. MM. 8, some 7.

8.57 MONCAYO, JOSÉ PABLO. Muros Verdes.
Green Walls has combination of purity and hypnotic forward motion. Tonal with very few accidentals. Textures wholly consistent within each section; each hand
usually has small step, legato single or parallel double
(thirds, fourths, or octaves) or triple notes. Linear
principle important, although LH may be acc. Unified
material spins out with few repetitions or cadences.
Varied rhythms have meter changes, irregular groupings, and polyrhythms. Tempos are Andante, lento,
and mostly allegro. (EMM, 1964, 14 pp.) MM.

8.58 NOËL-GALLON. Fleurs de Neige.
Snow Flowers is pleasant, animated salon piece with
sweetness so often found in French music. Flows easily under pianist's fingers. In first and last sections a
chromatic eighth-note melody is usually divided between
thumb of each hand, imbedded in flowing sixteenths.
Texture changes in middle section, so that bass chords
and treble arpeggiolike figurations are most important
elements. In c-sharp. Conservative. (In 8.2, 8 pp.)
Fngr, MM, Ped.

8.59 NØRGÅRD, PER. 9 Studies for Piano (1959).
Sensitivity in this twelve-tone work is revealed after
patient study. Discerning listeners can hear numerous
ostinatos which use an entire set or set fragment.
Melody pattern of the ostinatos is never the same length
as the rhythm pattern, or pattern may exist only in
rhythm or melody. Collection is organized as a total-
ity: procedures in Studies 1 and 2 have some relationship to Studies 8 and 9; 3 is related to 7, 4 to 6, and
5 stands alone in the middle. To supply some details
of this organization (a) the Prelude (Study 1) moves attacca to Trio I (Study 2), both using the same tone set
in the ostinato and the same treble melody, while Trio
II (Study 8) also moves attacca to Postlude (Study 9),
both using the same rhythmic pattern in the ostinato;
(b) Duo I (Study 3) uses a near-ostinato and a literal
ostinato as does Duo II (Study 7); (c) Counterlude I
(Study 4) uses an ostinato whose rhythmic pattern is a
different length from set fragment, as well as a fanci-

ful variation of the ostinato for the treble melody,
with similar construction used in Counterlude II (Study
6); and (d) Intermezzo (center Study 5) uses a long
double ostinato heard also in invertible counterpoint.
This organization (and more) will have to be sought
out by the performer as the basis for understanding
the collection's real expressiveness, as implied by the
beautiful beginning of the opening melody in harmon-
ics. Each study begins with a unison, octave, or
fifth, and ends with a fifth; entire Postlude is a marvellous play on fifths. (WH 4142, 1968, 13 pp.) MM,
some Ped. 8, some 7.

8.60 NYSTROEM, GÖSTA. Prelude Pastoral.
Expansive romantic Lentando. Clear tonal harmony
grows dense and dissonant with chromaticisms like
double inflections; harmonies become polychordal. Form
is A, becoming B, and returning to abbreviated A. A
is warmly lyrical, with RH outside-finger melody and
chords, and LH extended broken chords. Much in-
tensity and bravura in B with full chords and rapid LH
octaves, coupled writing, and RH passage work.
(Nord, 1960, 4 pp.) MM.

8.61 OHANA, MAURICE. Sonatine Monodique (1945).
Monodic Sonatina is splendidly fanciful. Resourceful
abstract play with tones. As title indicates, work is
entirely a single line--no acc. Single tones or their
octave doubling ingeniously used over a wide range,
usually without pedal. High degree of musicianship
needed for flexible chromatic lines and tempos. Allegretto con moto is approximately ABA in form. A has
two lyrical ideas, B has shorter note, non-legato writing with wide leaps. In the Vif, tones usually patter
back and forth rapidly between hands. Measures
marked "Lento a piacere" interrupt. The Andante is
rhapsodic with note values of much variety and one
tempo merging into another. Final Animé very effective, like a rondo with ingenious repetitions of material, including inversion of slower moving interlude.
(Bil, 1967, 17 pp.) 4 movements. 12 min. Some
MM & Ped. 8, some 7.

8.62 ORREGO, SALAS JUAN. Rustica, Op. 35 (1952).
Rustic overflows with attractive musical ideas. Witty
Vivo is energetic and effective. Nimble musical intel-
ligence assimilates many short ideas with splendid con-

fidence. Tonal, with all twelve tones freely used;
some polyharmony and fourth chords. Often linear
writing. Lively rhythms include meter changes, syncopations, and short ideas separated by rests. Varied
articulations and cross slurring. Dynamics change
abruptly. Wide keyboard range with such varied techniques as scales, forearm and hand staccatos on double
notes, rotary motion, and quick lateral shifts. Hands
equally emphasized. (PAU, 1954, 6 pp.) MM. Biog.

8.63 OVERTON, HALL. Polarities No. 1 (1958).
Thoughtful and substantial. Well-named, because polyharmonies, registers, linear lines, and contrary motion oppose each other. Sonorities include wide-
spaced chords through which pierce two steely, single
lines; lines usually conquer by erupting into cadenzalike passages. (In 6.4, 3 pp.) MM, Ped.

8.64 PAPAIOANNOU, JANNIS A. Oraculum.
Thoroughly contemporary, twelve-tone influenced work
of genuine musical conviction. At times a new set appears with each new measure; frequent rests occur.
Slow rubato tempo. Detailed dynamic directions. (In
7.1, 2 pp.) MM, some Ped. Biog.

8.65 PAPANDOPULO, BORIS. Dance Study (1930's).
Unabashedly brilliant virtuoso piece sounds more difficult than it is. Uses strong RH fingers and fairly
fast strong octaves in both hands. Hungarian minor
scale, as well as chromaticism. (In 7.2, 5 pp.)
MM. Biog.

8.66 PENTLAND, BARBARA. Fantasy (1962).
Splendidly imaginative and integrated Allegro in the
Schoenberg-Webern axis. Composer's concern for sonority and scherzo elements make the work fairly accessible. Combines tonality and twelve-tone principles.
Main tonality can be ascertained as B-flat because of
pedal at beginning and end; additionally, broad principle
of tonality is shown by reiteration of various non-ter-
tial chords. Twelve-tone principle is also treated
freely. Numerous harmonic sixths and ninths. Counting necessary for varied rhythms, which are not too
difficult. (At one point different tempos are indicated
for each hand, but one of the tempo and figures has
been established earlier.) Editing is thorough. Translation (p 7) is "veiled." (BMI, 1966, 9 pp.) MM. Ped.

8.67 PERSICHETTI, VINCENT. Eighth Piano Sonata, Op.
      41.
      Bright, optimistic music. Attractive melodies and
      lively irregular rhythms. Expert piano writing, with
      fine treatment of sonority. Dynamic level generally
      soft. Forms are clear, variations interesting. First
      movement characterizes "lightly" by staccatos, upper
      RH range, deft syncopations, and thin textures.
      Touches of polyharmony. Much variety of articulation.
      Marked "quietly," second movement's color is pastel.
      Bass has broken common chords supporting an equally
      wide-spaced melody. Much polyharmony. Final fast
      movement fertile with spontaneous ideas. Tonal har-
      monies freely use all twelve tones. Many thirds and
      sixths. Often broken chord staccato acc. Some osti-
      nato. (EV, 1955, 14 pp.) 3 movements. MM, some
      Ped. 8, some 6.

8.68 PERSICHETTI, VINCENT. Ninth Piano Sonata, Op.
      58.
      Serious work evocative of American optimism, hymns,
      and possibly folk tunes. Four movements joined. In
      the Moderato there are several clear ideas with intro-
      ductory material repeated at the end. Polyharmony
      used, as well as more traditional harmony, with voice
      leading important. Marked "cristallino," Allegro agil-
      ite movement sounds like a music box. Thirteenth
      chords from Alberti-like acc and chordal melody; also
      polyharmony. Arpeggios. Rotary motion. Larghetto
      is dolce, introspective. Pandiatonic harmonies in four-
      part chordal texture. Closing Allegro risoluto is tri-
      umphant in raucous mood and hornlike sonorities.
      Chords bound from register to register. (EV, 1963,
      15 pp.) 9 min. MM, some Ped.

8.69 POULENC, FRANCIS. XVème Improvisation.
      Very fast "capricious" yet lyrical music is masterfully
      unified. Fine tone study on small-step (leaps at stra-
      tegic points) treble melody using weaker fingers. RH
      also has double note acc usually alternating with mel-
      ody; LH usually has low bass tone and shifts quickly up
      to double notes or short secondary scale passages.
      Excellent for dynamic variety. In c, C, and a, with
      some contrast of melody in C. Harmonically and
      rhythmically conservative. (Sal, 1960, 5 pp.) MM.

8.70   POUSSEUR, HENRI.   Apostrophe et Six Réflexions
       (1964-1966).
       While the piano is played in the traditional manner,
       this Apostrophe and Six Reflections is among the most
       modern works reviewed in this Guide.   Concerning the
       Apostrophe, notes in 8.3 (where Apostrophe also ap-
       pears) report: "... an instructive example of the on-
       ward development of Webern's compositional principles,
       both as regards the structure of sound and the crea-
       tive use of silence." Rhythms are challenging: for
       example, meters in Apostrophe shift constantly be-
       tween 3/4, 4/8, 5/16, 5/8, 11/16, etc.; further, five
       beats may be compressed into time of four, beats sub-
       divided by triplets, etc.   The Six Reflections are titled,
       first being About Tempo with four mathematically re-
       lated metronome speeds, followed by About Phrases,
       About Dynamics, which range from pp to ff via large
       chords, About Touch, About Sonorities with half pedals
       and overtones activated from silently held lower tones
       and About Octaves.   Most Reflections quote literally
       from measures in Apostrophe, and several either re-
       peat measures or show close internal development.
       (UE 14773, 1968, 16 pp.)   MM, Ped.

8.71   POWELL, MEL.   Etude.
       Very contemporary.   Interesting combination of com-
       plexity and simplicity.   Form is introduction and
       theme with three variations.   Both twelve-tone and
       tonal.   In E-flat, leading tone and tonic ninth impor-
       tant; also tonic chord tones emphasized at variation
       endings.   Melody leaps.   Acc, including rapid groups,
       scampers about both in rhythms and pitches.   Some
       spots of unabashed virtuosity.   (In 6.4, 2 pp.)   MM.

8.72   QUINET, MARCEL.   Partita (1965).
       Three fast movements of idiomatic work are brilliant
       with perpetual motion staccatos and repeated disso-
       nances; lovely slow movements are post-impressionist.
       Variations on diminished or augmented octaves and in-
       versions are common to all movements.   Hands usual-
       ly equally emphasized.   Tonal by virtue of clear final
       chords.   Glittering first movement has high range fore-
       arm staccato broken chords and some skips.   Full tex-
       ture, exotic second movement often has accompanying
       ostinatos over low, long-sustained octaves.   Treble has
       brief rapid fragments and repeated tones with frequent
       diminished or augmented octaves.   Very fast, disso-

nant fifth movement is like a toccata. Quick hand alternations, often hand over hand, after two rotary motion, broken ninths or sevenths. Frequent double or
triple notes. Ends fff. (CBDM, 1966, 24 pp.) 5
movements. 10 min, 30 sec. MM. 8, some 6 & 7.

8.73 REYNOLDS, ROGER. Epigram and Evolution.
Twelve-tone pointillistic work. Leaps, often bridged
by grace notes, sometimes occur in rapid flurries.
Rhythm has remarkably clear notation, even while run-
ning the gamut in 2/4 meter from the very regular to
half beat divided by eight or two beats divided by three.
Clear notation has smaller notes than usual; extreme
pitches identified by letter names. Detailed dynamics.
Form of piece has set of twelve tones stated in the
Epigram; Evolution divided into brief, unified sections
from A through L. Endings after F and I are separated more than others, and piece ends with brief section comparable to Epigram. Sections G through I are
simpler, quieter, and more lyrical. I, the simplest,
is titled "Dogma:" appropriately here the set and its
transformations are stated most clearly. Five sections have many accelerandos, or are "improvisatory,"
or are to be played "very freely." (Pet P6618, 1968,
8 pp.) 6 min, 30 sec. MM, some Ped. *Biog.

8.74 RIVIER, JEAN. Stridences.
Presto "violent" number is a blatant show piece with
obvious devices skillfully used. Full range exploration with full textures. Strident it is from percussive
polyharmonies a half step, or other small interval,
apart. Parallel moving, common chords alternate rapidly between the hands or are played together. Excitement aroused by upward moving lines breaking into
clear octaves. Tension relieved by tunefulness, by
fine dynamic contrasts, and by a short, molto espressivo, Lento grave middle portion; however, brash excitement is never long suppressed. Splendid for
chords and forearm staccatos, and for developing
strength and endurance. (Noël, 1957, 12 pp.) MM.

8.75 ROCHBERG, GEORGE. Nach Bach (1966).
After Bach, subtitled "fantasy for harpsichord or piano," is, according to a communication from composer,
a "kind of commentary on J.S. Bach's Partita in e."
Four passages are boxed to indicate exact quotes from
the Partita; other rhythmically notated passages are

more or less taken from the Partita. Composer further writes that "Generally, the notation (indicates)
the nature of the pedaling," and "basically, where
notes are written out as tied, pedal should be applied."
Notation without meter or bar lines, and most often
without exact note lengths. Numerous directions like
"Bravura, begin at a moderate speed and gradually increase to prestissimo, wild" or "Gloriously, broad
(but don't drag)" suggest concern with which composer
helps performer in music where tasteful rhythmic authority is a prime requisite. Half or eighth notes
have beam to indicate groupings; eighth note groups
may also have diagonal beams to indicate acceleration
or ritard. Other notes are written in black with no
stems, horizontal line indicating general length to be
held. Length of rests often shown in seconds. Atonal; frequent broken or harmonic chords of a perfect
and augmented fourth. "Registration for the harpsichord by Igor Kipnis." (Pr, 1967, 16 pp.)

8.76 RODRIGO, JOAQUIN. Cuatro Estampas Andaluzas.
Four Andalusian Pictures are delightful, entertaining
pieces with Spanish allure. Idiomatic traditional piano
writing, with skillful variety of texture. Only moderately contemporary: slightly exotic out-of-key harmonies, delicate spark of seconds, and double inflections are present. Three pieces begin slow and end
fast. Seguidillas of the Devil is ABA in form. A has
harsh descriptive downward flourishes and insistent repeated note melody with arresting octave shifts. Much
hand alternation simulates castanets and guitar. Chromatic deftness of collection demonstrated by final
splash of concluding melodic minor scales in contrary
motion, with ascending scale also raising fourth and
fifth tones and descending also lowering fifth tone.
The slower, sultry copla (B) is lyrical. Little Boats
of Cadiz begins adagio with suspended dominant ninth
harmonies, sometimes moving parallel; ostinato also
included. Tempo shifts to Allegretto of solid content
and considerable impetus. Pianistic features include
easy rolling arpeggios, cross slurring, short Rh trills,
LH scale passages, quick octave shifts, etc. Translations are The Chanquete (type of fish) Vendor and Twi-
light over the Guadalquivir. (UME 19873, 1963, 29
pp.) Some Fngr, MM, some Ped. 8, some 6 & 7.

8.77 RUGGLES, CARL. Evocations (1937, 1941, 1943,
     1940, rev. 1954)
     Four Chants of compelling melodic lines amid complex
     harmonies, rhythms, and textures. Twelve-tone pro-
     cedures used. (See article in Journal of Music Theory
     for Spring, 1970.) Harmonies constantly activated by
     secondary contrapuntal lines. Notation of beat for flex-
     ible rhythms changes between quarter and eighth; beats
     divided by two through six freely mixed. Many poly-
     rhythms like four and three. MM markings for numer-
     ous tempo fluctuations. Smaller notes, to be held be-
     yond next pedal change, add texture fullness. Opening
     material always returns in some guise near the end.
     Detailed editing by John Kirkpatrick. In Largo I a
     single melodic line is amplified by coupling and then
     supported by bass and secondary melodic interest as
     dynamics increase to ff; texture thins again to single
     line with rapid repeated-tone acc. While each Evoca-
     tion includes a ff climax, III is intense from the begin-
     ning. Many strong gestures, stopped after one, two,
     or three measures. Each hand fully occupied. (AME,
     1956, 7 pp.) 4 pieces. Some Fngr, much MM & Ped.

8.78 SANTORO, CLAUDIO. Estudo N. 1.
     Allegro Etude No. 1 has obvious bombast from alter-
     nating-hand sonority; sounds more difficult than it is.
     Content is light weight. Suggestion of polyharmony,
     one hand usually on white keys, the other on black.
     RH uses parallel harmonic or broken fourth chords.
     Fine dynamic contrasts. Attractive Poco piu mosso
     section where texture thins to two lines and bass be-
     comes semi-ostinato. Smooth meter changes from
     simple 2/4 to compound 9/16 or 6/16; South American
     dance rhythm of three, three, and two near the end.
     Quick lateral shifts. (Ric-Br 2724, 1962, 6 pp.)
     Some Ped.

8.79 SANTORO, CLAUDIO. Estudo N. 2.
     Vivo Etude No. 2 will challenge rapid, strong fingers.
     Deviates from effective perpetual motion, coupled writ-
     ing for performer's rest and listener's variety. Som-
     ber introduction bides for time; then rampaging motion
     first breaks pace by LH second inversion triads moving
     contrary to RH. Fine slurring variety and irregular
     pitch pattern; mirror writing also used. LH acc keeps
     up chromatic motion in middle section, but RH is more
     lyrical in rhythm of three, three, and two, or three,

two, two, and one. First fast material returns, although more new material heard before longer repetition. Ends brilliantly with octaves. (Ric-Br 2746,
1962, 7 pp.)

8.80 SEARLE, HUMPHREY. Suite for Piano, Op. 29.
Variations, Nocturne, and Scherzo-Valse are witty and
pleasantly sophisticated twelve-tone music. Moderately full textures, with chords often effectively repeated.
Many sevenths and ninths. Flexible rhythms are only moderately contemporary. 10 Variations have much variety,
from frolicsome staccato flashes to presto brutal chord
slashes or expressive lento measures, etc. Whatever
the differences between variations, set is closely ad-
hered to; recognizable patterns are repeated. Outright
virtuosity often present. Frequent irregular rests.
Bass acc of lovely, serious Nocturne starts with wide
spans like Chopin. Becomes complicated with tremolo
figures and ingenious chromatic figurations; impressionistic in mood. (In 6.1, 12 pp.) 3 movements.
Some MM & Ped.

8.81 SILWESTROW, WALENTIN. 11 Serenade (1962).
Twelve-tone music, same set used throughout. Numerous meter changes. Dynamics, rarely exceeding f,
change frequently. Each movement moves attacca to
next. Short Allegro I uses brief flurries usually ending in a high B-flat as an upper pedal. Andantino 2
is poetic with warm, moderately full chords. Vivace
3 (moderately pointillistic, like 1) is scherzo in nature.
Single and double notes often repeated while a melody
flits about, interrupted by rests. Andantino opening
repeated at end. (In 6.7, 3-1/2 pp.) 3 movements.
MM, some Ped. Biog. 8, some 6.

8.82 SKALKOTTAS, NIKOS. 10 Piano Pieces (1940).
Music may impart a warm glow. Chromatic, non-
tonal, dense harmonies are individual and often quite
beautiful. Requires diligence to understand works and
audience must be "a discerning one." Textures very
full, wide reach used. Preface in German, with English facsimile by composer, and a biography. Taken
from 32 Piano Pieces. Andante Religioso well described by direction "harmonious." Numerous non-
routine appearances of motive from first measure are
supported by richly varied harmonies. They may appear as very full chords, unmeasured arpeggiolike

sweeps, fast melodic roulades or momentary secondary voices. Reverie in the New Style (also in 8.3) is
an introspective many-note work. Treble melody imbedded in rapid perpetual motion line of constant variety. Acc often moves from low to high in slower
motion, single notes. Many extensions. Damper pedal washes many tones together. Few dynamic marks.
Contrasting with another piece entitled Reverie in the
Old Style are its more numerous leaps in melody and
less traditional acc. Gavotte is lighter than most
pieces in the collection because of staccato notes and
thinner texture. Form is ABA. A is in three sections, the third repeating some of the first raised a
fifth, thus surprising with use of strong tonal interval.
In B the texture is often fuller, with two inner melodies for thumb-side of the hands alternating with
chords. Little Peasant March (also in 7.1) hints at
a popular basis, although much chromatic harmonic
thickness obscures. Homophonic texture. Fairly traditional piano writing. As usual, March includes a
Trio. (UE 12958, 1965, 44 pp.) Biog. 8, some 7.

8.83 STEVENS, HALSEY. Sonata No. 3 (1947-1948).
Effective, virile work with fine overall organization.
Shows mastery of thematic development. Balanced
mixture between the obvious and more obscure. Thoroughly contemporary tonal harmony. Full-texture writing, with frequent clarity of octaves, coupled writing
or thirds; in general, many double notes. Linear
counterpoint, when present, often involves double notes
in each hand. No meter signatures. Allegro non
troppo first movement has both declamatory and "dolce
expressivo" material. Rhythms "are plastic, in irregular groupings of two or three...." Frequent harmonic fourths and fifths; also octaves and thirds. Moderato con moto holds an interesting neutrality between
the tangibleness of outer movements. Has "... cross-
relations, simultaneous major-minor elements ...,"
etc. Final chord is minor ninth tonic chord in second
inversion. Climax is compelling, but expressiveness
must be sought. Rollicking Molto vivace rondo is high-
spirited and musically clear. Among prominent features are a three-beat figure in contrary motion, non-
patterned rapid passage work (sometimes in two voices)
and coupled writing. Includes scherzo and cantabile
elements. Short-long rhythms. Last three pages include a beautiful color change and ff poco piu larga-

mente closing measures. (AME, 1952, 26 pp.) 3
movements. 13 min, 32 sec. MM, some Ped.
*Anal. 8, some 7.

8.84 TAKÁCS, JENÖ. Sons et Silences, Op. 78 (1963-
     1964).
     Intriguing work, title taken literally. Both Sounds and
     Silences measured in seconds, indicated by distance
     between vertical lines drawn through separate horizon-
     tal line above the two staves. Each second is approxi-
     mate, as are note lengths; in fact, composer recom-
     mends deviations. This rhythmic notation surprisingly
     clear. Musical results obviously depend upon the per-
     former's rhythmic instinct. Fast passage work usual-
     ly brief. Row-influenced, with wide pitch and dynam-
     ic range. Directions in English and German. (Dob,
     1967, 7 pp.) MM, Ped.

8.85 THOMSON, VIRGIL. Nine Etudes, Set 2 (1940, 1951).
     Clever new use of old materials. Neo-romantic in
     spirit; hints of familiar airs help accessibility. Most
     Etudes are remarkably unified, focusing on a piano
     technique or tonal organization feature, or both.
     Double Sevenths uses only harmonic sevenths and only
     tones of C. Festive With Trumpet and Horn almost
     exclusively in lydian mode on A-flat, B-flat, and C.
     Uses forearm staccato strokes and rapid parallel
     chords. In a delightfully simple mood, Pivoting on the
     Thumb has continuous rippling motion of soft broken
     chords, either single or polychords, purely in C.
     Both hands have arpeggios or broken chords, also har-
     monic thirds, fifths, and sixths. Broken Arpeggios,
     subtitled The Waltzing Waters, has the sentiment of
     lavender and old lace. Perpetual motion in both hands.
     Only LH pivots on thumb. Splendid study for accuracy.
     Work uses only tones of D, G, and C. Ingenious Al-
     ternating Octaves has single tones alternating with oc-
     taves in both hands. Hands take turns leading in in-
     verted canon. Hands exchange keys in polytonal pure
     G-flat or G harmonies. Some skips. Fine for fore-
     arm (or hand) and finger staccato. (CF, 1954, 29 pp.)
     Some Fngr, MM, some Ped. 8, some 6 & 7.

8.86 TOMASI, HENRI. Danseuses de Degas.
     Degas Dancers is fanciful and frothy neo-romantic mu-
     sic, marked "elegant and melancholy." Waltz meas-
     ures interrupted by frequent stops, by notated change

to slower tempo or 2/4 meter, and by fast ascending
coupled scales. Rubato measures excellent for developing ingratiating style. Chromatic tonal harmonies
often have unresolved appoggiaturas and the like.
Widely arched spontaneous treble melody. (In 8.2, 6
pp.) Fngr, MM, Ped.

8.87 VALEN, FARTEIN. Intermezzo, Op. 36.
Intensely expressive Lento. Constantly polyphonic, usually in three voices; uses devices like invertible counterpoint. Because of the chromatic polyphony, harmony
is unimportant. Several distinct motives appear often.
4/4 meter includes many rhythms such as eighth notes
divided by three through six. Full keyboard range.
Non-standard rapid passage work uses weaker fingers.
Fast rotary motion on broken intervals. Resourceful
fingering needed for legato. (Ly 226, 1952, 4 pp.)

8.88 VERETTI, ANTONIO. Sonatina (1956).
Civilized music, as if to that manner born. Twelve-
tone and musical; some acknowledgment of tonality.
Has both transparent Italian traits of simple lyricism
and caprice, as well as brusque and more remote
moods. Masterful handling of form and thematic development. Allegro non troppo, marked "flowing," has
wit and variety. Familiar triadic elements used. Contrapuntal procedures slip in easily. Varied articulation. Aspiring Grave is severe, bringing splendid contrast. Alternates between chordal, contrapuntal, and
ff declamatory ideas. Presto, starting with one line
music of wide range and contrasting rhythms of two
and three, uses same tone set as Allegro. Later,
much is made of two-note, dissonant interval slurs,
repeated chords and parallel strands of thirds and
sixths. Rhythmically intricate because tones may enter
on second or third beat of fast triple measure. Both
outer movements build to impressive climaxes of progressive complexity. (Ric, 1957, 19 pp.) 3 movements. MM. 8, some 7.

8.89 WEINZWEIG, JOHN. Waltzling (1939).
Marvellous satire on the traditional waltz for discerning performer and listener. Ostinato of broken chromatic sixths holds down spirits of opening and closing
Allegro. Treble thirds start convulsively and late, then
break off defeated. However, passions surge in the
middle Presto where traditional waltz bass emerges,

chromatic thirds establish a longer line, and chromatic
scales rush to climaxes. B-flat appears to be the key
throughout, but allegretto ostinato starts and returns
to e. (In 8.1, 4 pp.) Biog. MM.

8.90 WOLPE, STEFAN. Early Piece for Piano (1924).
Superior, original work--ideas count rather than pian-
isms. Section tempos are Andante con moto, allegro,
poco meno mosso (a canon), and Andante repeated.
Particularly in Allegro section, touches of American
rural dance and jazz appear. Rhythms are complicated because of independence of two basic voices and
because each line is ornate. Syncopations are every-
where, particularly with main beat silent or with tone
tied through beat beginning. Ideas frequently end on
weak parts of beat; beats divided irregularly by two
through four. Harmonically conservative. (M&M,
1955, 8 pp.) MM.

8.91 ZABRACK, HAROLD. Scherzo.
Brilliant, appealing piece written in "hommage à Prokofieff." Obvious content sparkles with sudden modulations, polyharmonies, and audacious register changes.
Much articulation contrast and numerous dynamic
changes over a wide keyboard range. Techniques em-
ployed are hands crossing over each other, hand staccatos (particularly with triads), quick lateral shifts, ff
chords, as well as lyric tone. Hands equally emphasized. (B&H, 1967, 5 pp.) MM, Ped.

DATA FROM VOLUME I Pertinent to Volume II

3.23 DOLIN, SAMUEL. Old Dance (1953).
Haunting Andante semplice with skips in lovely melody.
Parallel seventh harmonies without third in section A,
included in section B; also double inflections of same
tone. Legato double notes in LH, often parallel fifths.
In f aeolian mode. (In 8.1, 1 p.) MM. Biog.

3.29 FLEMING, ROBERT. Strolling (1946).
Lovely simplicity. Most often in two voices, with LH
acc adding gentle coloring of ninths, sevenths or seconds to folklike melody. Acc has repeated two or three-
measure patterns. In aeolian mode on a. (In 8.1, 1
p.) MM. Biog.

4.9 International Library of Piano Music, Album 8.
Outstanding choice of composers and works. Covers
Impressionist and Twentieth Century periods. Available
only by purchasing entire set of nine albums. Six of
the nine works first published after 1950 are reviewed.
(See 3.11, 4.28, 4.68, 6.43 and 7.48.) Contains works
by Badings, Bartók, Benson, Blacher, Casella, Copland, Cowell, Debussy, Dello Joio, Dohnányi, Falla,
Fliarkowsky, Fortner, Glière, Gretchaninoff, Hindemith, Hovhaness, Ives, Jelinek, Kabalevsky, Khatchatur-
ian, Kodály, Krenek, Martin, Mennin, Miaskovsky,
Milhaud, Mompou, Palmgren, Piston, Poldini and
Prokofieff. (University Society, 268 pp.) 74 pieces,
32 composers. Some Fngr, MM, Ped. 4 & 6, some
3 & 5.

4.84 KASEMETS, UDO. Prelude, Op. 30, No. 2 (1952).
Lively. In words of composer, a meditation "... on
twelve-note serial, rhythmical, and metrical questions."
Twelve-tone basis doesn't preclude pattern repetitions
like tonic and dominant in C. Beyond notated 3/8
meter, there are two-beat patterns, as well as other
polyrhythms. Hands often quite far apart. (In 8.1,
2 pp.) MM. Biog.

4.122 RUSAGER, KNUDÅGE. Den Artige Dreng and Den
       Uartige Pige.
       The Well-Mannered Boy is sedate music in aeolian mode.
       Usually in two voices. Spontaneous Ill-Mannered Girl is
       "rather impudent" with sforzandos, staccatos and kaleido-
       scopic tonal harmonies. Middle section "smoother."
       End is "tangy again." Some coupled writing. (In 6.6, 1
       p & 1 p.) Some Fngr, MM. Biog. 4 & 5.

4.127 SAEVERUD, HARALD. Sonatina, Op. 30, No. 3.
       Aim of highest intent, impeccable craftsmanship. Sensi-
       tive, with refined subjectivity. Tonal, with free use of
       all twelve tones. In two-part texture. Allegretto grazi-
       oso securely directs ebb and flow of tension and release
       through ritards, accelerandos, and changes of tempo.
       Andante's RH melody heard twice with different harmoni-
       zations: second time adds bass range with surprising in-
       toning of tonic tone. Much subtle detail. (In 6.5, 3 pp.)
       2 movements. MM. 4 & 5.

5.1 DESCAVES, LUCETTE, ed. Les Contemporains
     (Deuxième Recueil).
     Second Collection of The Contemporaries has pianistical-
     ly deft works, useful for exploring accidentals within ton-
     ality. Five are reviewed (see 5.48, 5.116, 5.131, 6.10,
     and 6.35)--others usually too conservative. Preface, in
     French, by Daniel Lesur "for parents" and "for students."
     Music by Aubin, Auric, Bondeville, Delannoy, Dutilleux,
     Gallois-Montbrun, Hoeree, Revel, Rivier, Schmit, and
     Yvain. Titles usually in French, English, German, and
     Spanish. (Bil, 1950, 37 pp.) 11 pieces, 11 composers.
     Fngr, some MM, Ped. 5 & 6.

5.3 International Library of Piano Music, Album 9.
     Outstanding choice of composers and works. Covers Im-
     pressionist and Twentieth Century periods. Available on-
     ly by purchasing entire set of nine albums. All works
     first published within the time scope of this study are re-
     viewed. (See 5.136 and 7.89.) Contains works by Ravel,
     Rebikoff, Reger, Riegger, Schönberg, Scriabin, Sessions,
     Shostakovitch, Smith, Sorokine, Stravinsky, Sydeman,
     Toch, Turina, Villa Lobos, and Webern. (University So-
     ciety, 1967, 181 pp.) 40 pieces, 16 composers. Some
     Fngr, MM & Ped. 5 & 7.

5.5 Svenska Albumblad 1962.
     Swedish Albumleaves, commissioned by publisher,

were written in 1962. Ten works reviewed. (See
5.28, 5.72, 5.83, 5.158, 6.79, 6.80, 6.93, 6.129,
and 7.31.) As pointed out in foreword, pieces are
quiet and of an inward expressiveness, with one ex-
ception. Most are mildly contemporary, with somewhat lavish piano sound. Contains music by Carlstedt,
De Frumerie, Eklund, Hallnäs, Johanson, Karkoff, v.
Koch, Larsson, Liljefors, Linde, Rosenberg, and
Wirén. Foreword in Swedish, titles in Swedish and
Italian. (P 8 & 12.) (Geh, 1962, 20 pp.) 12 pieces,
12 composers. Some MM & Ped. 5 & 6, some 7.

5.15 BECKWITH, JOHN. The Music Room (1951).
Serious work of beautiful logic. Compositional skill
shown in transitions of first Andantino to Piu allegro
and back again. Compelling contrapuntal lines. Prominent legato double notes, mostly sixths. May be E-
flat or e-flat. No key signature. (In 8.1, 2 pp.)

5.79 LESUR, DANIEL. L'Armoricaine.
Cantabile Woman from Brittany tastefully set, with in-
itial dependence on fingers alone and fuller setting with
pedal later. Often coupled writing. Legato repeated
tones. Modal influences in melody. Free material of
appropriate character used between appearances of folk
melody. (In 8.2, 2 pp.) Fngr, some Ped.

5.82 LIDHOLM, INGVAR. Sonatin (1947).
Fresh twists to familiar materials in two-voice texture. In g. Neo-classic and convincing. Opening
Marsch swaggers gracefully with dotted rhythms and
mildly angular melody. Pastoral is simple and lovely.
In treble register, with piquant chromatic coloring in
LH acc. Like other movements, Rondo is musically
transparent. High spirits denoted by staccatos and accents, but middle section more reserved. Frequent
meter changes. (In 6.6, 3 pp.) 3 movements. MM.
Biog. 5, some 4.

5.103 PAPINEAU-COUTURE, JEAN. Valse I and II (1943,
1944).
Refined. First of the Two Waltzes marked modéré.
Prominent are accompanying fourth chords; excursions
in middle section into many flats, from a. Second
Waltz moves fast and flexibly. In C, with minor dominant often used; delightful modulations in middle section. RH often has three-note chords, LH usually

single notes which move lower for chord root.   (In
8.1, 2 pp.) Some Fngr, MM & Ped.

5.119 SAEVERUD, HARALD. Sonatina, Op. 30, No. 5.
Inventive music, "quasi una fantasia," communicates
well. Movements connected without pause. Allegretto
is exquisitely tender with very fanciful ending. Much
use of opening motive. Moderato has double note LH
acc; in contrast, rest of Sonatina usually only two
voices. Bright spirited Allegro assai is soft, "but
marked," and non legato. Has sudden outbursts.
Closing Allegretto has delicate single note alternation
between hands, with material from first and second
movements. (In 6.5, 5 pp.) 4 movements. MM.
Biog.

5.126 SAUGUET, HENRI. La Chanson du Soir.
Evening Song is an expert pastel, colors blurred together by pedal ("change each measure"). RH leads
in two-voice texture. Melody often suspended on added
second, while acc touches added sixth. Conservative.
(In 8.2, 2 pp.) Fngr, MM, Ped.

5.151 TSUKATANI, Y. Sakura Sakura, Edo Komoriuta,
    Chūgokuchihō No Komoriuta, Hirosaki Shishimai-
    Odori, Yagi Bushi and Aizu Bandaisan.
Direct appeal, whether quiet or brilliant. As usual,
harmonic seconds, fourths and fifths (not thirds)
prominent. Melodies in a two-half step pentatonic
scale, with first three on same pitch. Lovely Cherry
Blossom, Cherry Blossom (p 6) is "like a nocturne."
Between simple statements of melody whole step apart
there are flourishes of exotically colored broken treble
chords. Lullaby from Edo (p 8) and Lullaby from
District of Chogoku (p 9) are most sensitive. In both,
second setting of melody imaginatively varied. First
marked Adagio, but may be "andante or lento;" second
directed to be "rubato." Lion Dance from Hirosako
(p 24) and Melody from Yagi (p 26) are brilliant, extrovert works propelled by varied percussive thrusts.
In first, LH forearm stabs give drum beats, to which
is added RH in second number. Latter is indeed
"healthy," "humorous," and "capricious." RH has
rapid repeated tones. Allegro moderato Mount Aizu
Bandai Dance (p 28) aims to help people to "work
well;" it is "clean and simple." Melody has single
tones, or is coupled. Each hand alternates in simple

rhythmic acc using hand staccatos. (In 6.3, 2 pp, 1 p, 1 p, 2 pp, 2 pp, & 3 pp.) Anal. 5, 4, 5, 7, 7, & 5.

5.153 WAGNER-RÉGENY, RUDOLF.   Zwei Klavierskizzen. Two Piano Sketches use obvious twelve-tone technique. Same set used for both works: first Sketch, in original order, second Sketch in retrograde order, returning to original order at end. Emphasis given to first or last tone of set for tonal impression. Hands treated equally. Ninth reach necessary. Expressive melody in I. Texture has much variety. Three different double notes often used for acc. Fine climaxes. II has clear phrases, each phrase stating set once. Wide range melody alternates with fanfare of ninths. Invertible counterpoint. (In 8.3, 3 pp.) Biog.

GLOSSARY

(Terms not in Harvard Brief Dictionary of Music)

ARTICULATION. Refers, in a narrow sense, to staccato and/or legato manner of performance; more inclusively, nearly synonymous with phrasing.

COUNTER-MELODY. An independent melody, but secondary to the most important melody.

COUPLED WRITING. Melody doubled by second hand, usually at the octave. Coupled two-part writing has double notes in one hand duplicated by the other hand.

DOUBLE INFLECTION. A tone and its chromatic alteration sound together, or in immediate succession in different voices. Same as cross relation.

DOUBLE NOTES. Two different simultaneous notes in one hand.

EXTENDED INTERVALS, or EXTENSIONS. Wide-spaced intervals, where stretching between adjacent fingers is needed.

FIVE-FINGER POSITION. Narrowly, each finger is on consecutive diatonic tones; more broadly, no thumb-under is used.

GESTURE. A particularly striking rhythmic or melodic contour.

KEY SIGNATURE OMITTED. Indicates that, while music is tonal, keys change so frequently or so many accidentals are used, that printing is more easily read when notes are natural unless otherwise indicated.

138

METERS, VARIABLE. Changing meters, such as 2/8 to
    3/8 to 4/8 to 5/8. Meter signatures may be omit-
    ted.

MIRROR WRITING. One line moves opposite or contrary to
    another; c up to e would be reflected by c down to
    a-flat.

MODAL INTERCHANGE. Tonal center remains, but modes
    are changed.

NON-TONAL. Some common triads or important repeated
    single tones are present, but no specific tonality can
    be determined.

OFFBEAT. Part of a measure other than the principally ac-
    cented one; for example, second or fourth beat in a
    4/4 measure, or between usual beats.

ONE-LINE MUSIC. Melody only, no accompaniment.

POLYHARMONY, or POLYTONALITY. Two (or more)
    identifiable harmonies, or tonalities, sounding at
    same time.

RAGA. A melody-type in Hindu music.

ROTARY MOTION. Forearm rotates from left to right, or
    the reverse.

SCALE, DOUBLE HARMONIC. Like the major mode, but
    with lowered second and sixth tones.

SCALE, HUNGARIAN MAJOR. Like the mixolydian mode,
    but with raised second and fourth tones.

SCALE, HUNGARIAN MINOR. Like the aeolian mode, but
    with raised fourth and seventh tones.

SCALE, LYDIAN MINOR. Like the lydian mode, but with
    lowered sixth and seventh tones.

SCALE, MAJOR LOCHRIAN. Like the major mode, but with
    lowered fifth, sixth, and seventh tones.

SCALE, OVERTONE. Like the lydian mode, but with low-
    ered seventh tone.

SCALE, SUPER LOCHRIAN. Like the phrygian mode, but
  with lowered fourth and fifth tones.

SCALE, SYNTHETIC. Any scale formation not frequently
  found.

SECUNDAL HARMONY. Chords based on the interval of the
  second.

SEGMENT OF TWELVE-TONE SET. Tones selected from
  the twelve-tone set and used as a unit of organization.

SET TRANSFORMATION. Order of tones in a twelve-tone set
  is changed, such as from the original order to its inversion, or to retrograde, or to retrograde inversion.

SHORT-LONG RHYTHM. Rhythmic unit like an eighth note followed by a quarter note; less common than the reverse.

STACCATO, FINGER. Finger moves as a unit from the hand-
  knuckle for staccato touch

STACCATO, FOREARM. Hand and fingers move as a unit from
  the elbow joint for staccato touch.

STACCATO, HAND. Hand and fingers move as a unit from the
  wrist joint for staccato touch.

TEXTURE, FULL. Sound has many tones, often in a wide range.
  Opposed to thin texture, where few tones are used.

TONALITY, REMOTE. Tonal, but vague; perhaps a bass tone
  (tonic) is reiterated, but other tones are unrelated.

TRIADS, FREELY ASSOCIATED. Succession of common triads
  without regard for tonality.

TWELVE-TONE SET. Same as twelve-tone series or twelve-
  tone row.

UNMETERED. Meter (or time) signature is omitted; note values
  usually present, but there are no patterns of values.

VOICE. A single melodic line. Same as part.

INDEX TO MUSICAL AND PIANISTIC FEATURES

141

8. 5, 6, 8, 9, 10, 15, 17, 18, 19, 21, 25, 26, 30, 3̄1, 32, 33, 43, 54, 56, 58, 61, 65, 76, 79, 80, 82, 86, 87, 89.

CLUSTER CHORDS 6. 3, 8, 12, 40, 58, 70, 71, 78, 89, 100, 101, 125̄, 129, 163, 168; 7. 9, 20, 28, 45, 51, 52, 68, 72, 78, 79, 83; 8. 1̄4, 17, 23, 28, 31, 36, 53.

CONSERVATIVE 6. 6, 22, 26, 29, 31, 34, 51, 57, 58, 104, 109, 1̄10, 132, 150; 7. 38, 40, 60, 69; 8. 33, 58, 69.

COUPLED WRITING 6. 15, 16, 17, 21, 23, 26, 32, 36, 46, 48, 51, 54̄, 58, 67, 83, 87, 91, 95, 97, 99, 104, 107, 108, 116, 129, 148, 150, 161, 164, 165, 170; 7. 18, 23, 25, 31, 32, 40, 42, 43, 45, 49, 52, 58, 5̄9, 60, 61, 65, 68, 71, 72; 8. 17, 24, 29, 31, 37, 48, 49, 56, 60, 77, 79, 83, 86̄.

DISSONANCE 6. 24, 41, 45, 57, 60, 78, 96, 97, 100, 106, 119, 126̄, 137, 148, 152, 164; 7. 5, 21, 40, 53, 67, 68, 71, 79, 83, 86; 8. 9, 1̄2, 18, 28, 29, 48, 52, 60, 72, 88.

DOTTED RHYTHM 6. 20, 24, 56, 57, 115, 117, 126, 131, 132, 152; 7̄. 5, 17, 22, 31, 70; 8. 13, 91.

DOUBLE NOTES or CHORDS, BROKEN see BROKEN DOUBLE NOTES or CHORDS

DOUBLE NOTES, HARMONIC (block) 6. 13, 15, 16, 17, 28, 32, 42, 43, 44, 50, 55, 77̄, 84, 92, 97, 99, 107, 110, 112, 115, 119, 125, 129, 135, 136, 137, 138, 144, 148, 158, 167, 168; 7. 12, 19, 28, 29, 30, 33, 40, 42, 47, 53, 54, 62, 6̄3, 65, 68, 71, 74, 78, 79, 81, 83, 84, 85, 95; 8. 6, 9, 11, 13, 15, 16, 18, 21, 26, 28, 29, 35, 43̄, 44, 48, 51, 54, 55, 56, 59, 62, 66, 67, 69, 72, 81, 83, 85, 88, 89.

DOUBLE NOTES or CHORDS, LEGATO see LEGATO DOUBLE NOTES or CHORDS

DYNAMIC VARIETY 6. 11, 12, 20, 34, 48, 53, 76, 82, 100, 139, 149, 1̄53, 160, 164; 7. 13, 14, 22, 34, 36, 45, 49, 74, 94; 8. 32, 38, 4̄1, 62, 64, 69,

INDEX TO COMPOSERS AND COMPOSITIONS

ORDERING INSTRUCTIONS

Music described in this Guide may be had from your local music dealer or from the following central sources:

JOSEPH BOONIN, INC.
P. O. Box 2124
So. Hackensack, N. J. 07606
Tel. (201) 488-1450

de KEYSER MUSIC
6737 Hollywood Blvd.
Hollywood, Calif. 90028
Tel. (213) 465-5035

When ordering from either of the above two dealers, music may be described by the given index number only (6.1). Be sure to specify quantities greater than one, and the desired shipping method. Ways of shipping, from slowest, most economical to fastest, most expensive are: Special Fourth Class Rate (Book Rate); Special Handling; Special Delivery; Air Mail; and Air Mail Special Delivery. Orders which do not specify preferred method will be sent Special Fourth Class Rate.

Orders totalling less than $25.00 will be shipped prepaid and billed on open account. Those amounting to more than $25.00 will be answered by return mail with an itemized invoice, and the music will be shipped immediately upon receipt of remittance of the total.

Prices for individual items will be given on request. Include self-addressed stamped envelope.

Allow three weeks delivery time for music published in the U.S.A. or Canada; music published overseas may in many cases require rather more time. Any item requiring more than ninety days to supply will be subject to a report contingent on publisher's information. Items undergoing a permanent change in availability will be reported on receipt of order. Music sent on definite order is not returnable unless defective in manufacture or incorrectly filled on order.

PUBLISHER INFORMATION

Abbreviation	Publisher	U.S. Agent
AE	Amberson Enterprises	GS
Al	G. Alsbach & Co.	Pet
AME	American Music Edition	Joseph Boonin, Inc.
AMP	Associated Music Publishers, Inc.	
A&S	Ahn & Simrock	Sal
Aug	Augener, Ltd.	Galx
Bär	Bärenreiter-Verlag	
Barry	Barry & Cia	B&H
B&B	Bote & Bock	AMP
Beek	Beekman Music, Inc.	Pr
Bel-M	Belwin-Mills	
B&H	Boosey & Hawkes, Inc.	
Bil	Editions Billaudot	Pr
BMI	Berandol Music, Ltd.	AMP
Bong	Edizioni Bongiovanni	Bel-M
Br&H	Breitkopf & Härtel	AMP
BrB	Broude Bros Music	
B&VP	Broekmans & Van Poppel	Pet
CBDM	Belgian Centre of Music Documentation	HE
CF	Carl Fischer, Inc.	
Chap	Chappell & Company, Inc.	
Chap-L	Chappell & Company, Ltd., London	
Ches	J. & W. Chester, Ltd.	

Abbreviation	Publisher	U.S. Agent
Chou	Editions Choudens (see Bil)	
Cos	Editions Costallat (see Bil)	
Der	Derry Music Company	Sha
Dit	Oliver Ditson Company	Pr
Dob	Ludwig Doblinger Musikverlag	AMP
Don	Stitching Donemus	Pet
Du	Duchess Music Corporation	MCA
Dur	Durand & Cie	EV
Elk	Elkin & Company, Ltd.	Galx
EMB	Editio Musica Budapesta	B&H
EMM	Ediciones Mexicanas de Musica, A.C.	SMP
EMT	Editions Musicales Transatlantiques	Pr
Esc	Editions Max Eschig	AMP
EV	Elkan-Vogel Company	Pr
Faz	Musik Fazer	
FC	Franco Colombo	Bel-M
Fox	Sam Fox Publishing Company	
G&C	G&C Music Corporation	Chap
Gal	Galliard, Ltd.	Galx
Galx	Galaxy Music Corporation	
Geh	Carl Gehrmans Musikförlag	
Gen	General Music Publishing Co., Inc.	Frank Distributing Company
	Gerig, Musikverlage Hans (see HG)	
GS	G. Schirmer, Inc.	
GVT	Gordon V. Thompson, Limited	
	Hansen, Wilhelm, Musik-forlag (see WH)	
Har	The Frederick Harris Music Co., Ltd.	
HE	Henri Elkan Music Publisher	
Hein	Heinrichshofen's Verlag	Pet
Hel	Helios Music Edition	Mark Foster

Abbreviation	Publisher	U.S. Agent
Heu	Heugel & Cie	Pr
HG	Musikverlage Hans Gerig	MCA
HiP	Highgate Press	Galx
Hin	Hinrichsen Edition, Ltd.	Pet
HL	Henry Lemoine & Cie	
HP	Henmar Press	Pet
IMI	Israel Music Institute	B&H
IMP	Israel Music Publications	MCA
IVi	Irmaos Vitale S/A	Lawrence J. Greene 200 W. 57th St. N.Y.C. 10019
JF	J. Fischer & Bro.	Bel-M
Jos	Joshua Corporation	Gen
JW	Josef Weinberger	Pr
Led	Alphonse Leduc & Cie	
Leeds-NY	Leeds Music Corporation	MCA
Leeds-C	Leeds Music (Canada) Limited	MCA
	Lemoine & Cie, Henry (see HL)	
LG	Lawson-Gould Music Pub., Inc.	GS
Lit/Pet	Henry Litolff's Verlag	Pet
LR	Lee Roberts Music Publications	
Ly	Harald Lyche & Co's Musikforlag	Pet
MCA	MCA Music	
McK	Peter McKee Music Co.	Wat
Mer	Merion Music, Inc.	Pr
Merc	Mercury Music Corporation	Pr
Metr	Editions Metropolis	HE
Mil-L	Mills Music, London	
Mil-NY	Mills Music, Inc.	Bel-M
MJQ	MJQ	
M&M	McGinnis & Marx	

Abbreviation	Publisher	U.S. Agent
Mrk	Edward B. Marks Music Corporation	
Muz	Muzyka	MCA
Noël	Pierre Noël Editeur (see Bil)	
Noet	Otto Heinrich Noetzel Verlag	Pet
Nord	AB Nordiska Musikförlaget	
Norsk	Norsk Musikforlag A/S	
Nov	Novello & Company Ltd.	Bel-M
NVMP	New Valley Music Press of Smith College	
Ongaku	Ongaku-No-Tomo Sha Corporation	
Orc	Orchesis Publications	
Oxf	Oxford University Press	
Pan	Panton	B&H
PAU	Pan American Union	SMP
Peer	Peer International Corporation	SMP
Pet	C. F. Peters Corporation	
Pr	Theodore Presser Company	
PWM	Polskie Wydawnictwo Muzyczne	Mrk
Ric	G. Ricordi & Co., Milan	Bel-M
Ric-Ba	Ricordi Americana, Buenos Aires	Bel-M
Ric-Br	Ricordi Brasileira, Sao Paulo	Bel-M
Ric-L	G. Ricordi, London	Bel-M
Ron	Rongwen Music, Inc.	BrB
Row	R. D. Row Music Co., Inc.	CF
Sal	Editions Salabert	
SB	Summy-Burchard Company	
Scho	Schott & Co., Ltd.	Bel-M
ScS	B. Schott's Söhne	Bel-M
SF	Schott Frères	Pet
Sha	Shawnee Press, Inc.	
Shv	Statnehudobne vydavelstve (see Sup)	

171

Abbreviation	Publisher	U.S. Agent
Sim	N. Simrock	AMP
SMP	Southern Music Publishing Co. , Inc.	
Sov	Soviet Composers	
St&B	Stainer & Bell Ltd.	Galx
Sup	Editio Supraphon	B&H
Tem	Alec Templeton	Sha
UE	Universal Edition	Pr
UWP	University of Washington Press	Galx
UME	Union Musical Española	AMP
VMP	Valley Music Press of Smith College	
Wat	Waterloo Music Company Limited	
	Weinberger, Joseph (see JW)	
Weint	Weintraub Music Company	
WH	Wilhelm Hansen, Musik-forlag	GS
Zen	Edition Zen-On	
Zer	Edizioni Suvini Zerboni	MCA